A Sneetch
Is a Sneetch
and Other
Philosophical Discoveries

A Sneetch Is a Sneetch
and Other Philosophical Discoveries

Finding Wisdom in Children's Literature

Thomas E. Waternberg

Illustrations by JoyKinigstein

WILEY-BLACKWELL

A John Wiley & Sons, Ltd., Publication

This edition first published 2013
© 2013 John Wiley & Sons Inc

Wiley-Blackwell is an imprint of John Wiley & Sons, formed by the merger of Wiley's global
Scientific, Technical and Medical business with Blackwell Publishing.

Registered Office
John Wiley & Sons Ltd, The Atrium, Southern Gate, Chichester, West Sussex, PO19 8SQ, UK

Editorial Offices
350 Main Street, Malden, MA 02148-5020, USA
9600 Garsington Road, Oxford, OX4 2DQ, UK
The Atrium, Southern Gate, Chichester, West Sussex, PO19 8SQ, UK

For details of our global editorial offices, for customer services, and for information about how to
apply for permission to reuse the copyright material in this book please see our website at
www.wiley.com/wiley-blackwell.

The right of Thomas E. Wartenberg to be identified as the author of this work has been asserted in
accordance with the UK Copyright, Designs and Patents Act 1988.

Library of Congress Cataloging-in-Publication Data
Wartenberg, Thomas E.
    A sneetch is a sneetch and other philosophical discoveries : finding wisdom in children's
literature / Thomas E. Wartenberg.
        pages cm
    Includes bibliographical references and index.
    ISBN 978-0-470-65678-5 (cloth : alk. paper) – ISBN 978-0-470-65683-9
(pbk. : alk. paper) 1. Children's literature--History and criticism. 2. Philosophy in literature.
3. Children--Books and reading. 4. Knowledge, Theory of, in literature. I. Title.
    PN1009.A1W296 2013
    809′.89282 – dc23
                                                                        2012050385

Cover image: Illustration by J.H. Dowd, 1923. Reproduced with permission of Punch Limited
Cover design by http://www.simonlevy.co.uk

Typeset in 10.5/13pt Minion by Laserwords Private Limited, Chennai, India
Printed in Singapore by Ho Printing Singapore Pte Ltd

2 2013

In memory of Gareth B. Matthews
who first showed me the wisdom in picture books

Go to *www.teachingchildrenphilosophy.
for worksheets on the books   org
— Frog + Toad "Dragons & Giants" (Virtues)
        — Can people be brave + scared
                        at the same time...

Contents

** + whats the big idea program.com

Acknowledgments

This book has benefitted from the support and contributions of many people. First, I want to thank Abby Goodnough, the *New York Times* reporter who wrote a wonderful article about my work introducing elementary school children to philosophy (accessible on www.teachingchildrenphilosophy.org). While reading *Big Ideas for Little Kids*, the book in which I describe my program, she commented on how the chapters in which I discussed the picture books we use in elementary school classrooms really helped her understand philosophy. It was like an introduction to philosophy, she remarked. A light went off in my head and the present book is the outcome of my illumination.

The students in my first-year seminar, Approaching Philosophy through Picture Books, in the fall of 2010, convinced me that this was a book worth writing. The excitement and delight they had thinking philosophically about picture books confirmed my belief in this project, and I am very appreciative of their help in thinking about the philosophical issues in the books we discussed together.

I am truly grateful for the enthusiasm with which my editor at Wiley-Blackwell, Jeff Dean, whom I feel privileged to call a friend, greeted this project. Not only did he help me formulate my ideas, but Jeff also hung in with me as I struggled to find an appropriate style with which to write the book. Although I am the author of a number of philosophy books that I thought were written in a popular style, he showed me that I had a long way to go to reach the right degree of accessibility. Whether he succeeded, only the readers of this book can judge.

A number of people read various parts of the book. My good friend, Lewis Popper, read an earlier version and helped me make it less arcane. My son, Jake, read a number of chapters in the penultimate version of the manuscript and gave excellent suggestions that have improved the book.

Kate Thomson-Jones and Meredith Michaels also gave me useful feedback. Anna Faherty of Strategic Content went over some of my manuscript with a fine-toothed comb and helped shape the final manuscript. Difficult as her suggestions were for me to accept, the book bears evidence of their utility. And the Facebook friends of Teaching Children Philosophy helped me figure out a title that I hope captures the spirit of this book.

Joy Kinigstein was great to work with. Her illustrations shed fresh light on the puzzling situations envisioned in the chapter subtitles.

Without the support of my wife, Wendy Berg, I would not have been able to give this book the attention it needed. She discussed many of my ideas with me, read a great deal of the manuscript, debated various suggestions for the book's title, and generally gave me invaluable suggestions about how to improve this book. I am immensely grateful for all that she has done for me in seeing this book to fruition.

I dedicate this book to the memory of the person who not only taught me that children were natural-born philosophers, but who also showed me that it was possible to live a life infused with the Socratic spirit, the late Gareth B. Matthews. Gary's patience, generosity, intelligence, humor, and keen appreciation of life serve as a model for me in more than just a professional sense. I imagine him reading this book with a smile on his face and a twinkle in his eye. I regret that he did not live to have that opportunity.

Lower Highland Lake
Goshen, Massachusetts
August 31, 2012

"Why? Why? Why?"

Children, Philosophy, and Picture Books

Parents are all too aware of their children's innate inquisitiveness, having been frequently greeted with the repeated refrain: "Why?", "Why?", "Why?" When you are trying to finish the week's grocery shopping, you just don't have time for your kids' questions: "Mom, why do we have to pay for food?" "Daddy, if people don't have money to pay for food, is it all right for them to steal what they need to survive?" Enough. You've got a thousand things to do before dinner. You just can't be bothered answering so many difficult questions.

These children's harried parents may not realize that their kids' quest for understanding allies them with philosophers, whose own determined search for answers can be just as annoying to friends, colleagues, and family. The last thing you want to hear when you are late for a doctor's appointment is your philosopher-friend's query, "Have you ever stopped to consider that time may not be real?" Kids and philosophers seem determined to place obstacles in our way as we try to complete the various tasks life demands.

When you reflect upon this tendency in more leisurely circumstances than your weekly trip to the grocery store affords, you'll realize that these annoying tendencies are the result of both children and philosophers trying to understand puzzling features of their – and our – lives. The reason that they both keep asking "Why?" is that they refuse to skip over those confounding aspects of reality that most of us ignore as we attend to our everyday concerns.

A Sneetch Is a Sneetch and Other Philosophical Discoveries: Finding Wisdom in Children's Literature, First Edition. Thomas E. Wartenberg. Illustrations © Joy Kinigstein.
© 2013 John Wiley & Sons, Inc. Published 2013 by John Wiley & Sons, Inc.

Not every question a child asks is philosophical. Many times, they are wondering about how things work and the answers are essentially technical or scientific. The paradigmatic child's question, "Why is the sky blue?", might seem to be asking an adult to trot out the laws of refraction, for these do explain why the sky is *blue*. However, even in what appears a request for scientific information, a philosophical puzzle is concealed, viz. *What type of thing is the sky?* Although we ordinarily may talk as if there were a sort of painted dome around the earth that we call "the sky," we all know that there is no such thing. So a child's question might push us to ask, "Does the sky actually exist?" And if, as I have been suggesting, it doesn't, at least in the form we naively take it to, we might begin to wonder how we can be aware of something that doesn't really exist. Behind many of the questions that children ask, there lie deep questions about the nature of the world they – and we – inhabit, questions that most of us adults have put aside, perhaps because we have no clear answers to them.

Writers of great picture books are well attuned to the features of the world that baffle young children. Since many of these bewildering puzzles also befuddle philosophers, picture books frequently focus on philosophical issues. This book shows how many of the essential problems of philosophy are made tangible by the picture books your children – and you – know so well. In turn, much of the enjoyment that picture books deliver comes from the inventive ways in which writers and illustrators present genuine philosophical puzzles that intrigue children and adults alike.

What you'll find in these pages is an introduction to a wide range of philosophical concepts and questions, from all the distinct areas of philosophy. Philosophers concern themselves with many different types of questions: Is there a correct way to act in even the most trying of circumstances? Is it all right to harm natural things when doing so helps people? How much can you change something before it no longer is the same thing? Are all people essentially the same? If you think that you know something, does that mean that people who disagree with you are wrong? Such questions are the stuff of philosophy and you'll see how picture books also puzzle over them.

Introducing Philosophy

My presentation of the questions raised by children's picture books in the following chapters will introduce you to many different philosophical questions and areas of investigation. Now, however, I want to say something about philosophy in general. It will be useful to have an idea of what philosophy is as you delve into the more specific issues presented in the following chapters.

Most of the time, as you live your life, you are engaged in the various activities that make it up. When you are grocery shopping, for example, you pause to remember what you need to buy or which type of vegetable looks freshest. You are thinking, but your thinking is oriented towards your task of shopping. Same thing holds when you are balancing your checkbook. You are thinking about numbers, indeed likely puzzling over them, but only in so far as they help you see whether you and your bank agree about how much money is in your account.

Sometimes, however, maybe when you are shopping, or when you are struggling to get the checkbook to balance, or even during those rare moments when you don't seem to have anything special to do, you disengage from those ordinary activities and reflect upon why you are doing what you are doing or what the activity you were pursuing really amounts to. You might wonder, say, whether there isn't more to life than getting up each day, sending your kids off to school, cleaning the house, buying the groceries, greeting your kids as they arrive home from school, getting dinner ready, eating, cleaning up, and putting them – and yourself – to bed. Or you might wonder whether the numbers that float before your eyes as you struggle with your bank statement are real, since they seem very different from the computer and bank statement sitting in front of you, for those two things have a physical existence in a way that pure numbers do not.

At such a moment in your life, you are engaging in philosophical reflection about your life. What makes your thinking *philosophical* is that it has become detached from pursuing a specific activity, like grocery shopping, and focused on the nature and meaningfulness of it. Philosophy begins where our ordinary concerns are held in abeyance. It involves reflective thinking, thinking that takes as its topic the things we normally take for granted, and assume to be comprehensible and fully intelligible.

The reflective thinking that philosophy employs is quite different from the type of thinking involved in our normal activities, even if they both are concerned with the same things. When, to continue with one of the examples I have been using, you are balancing your checkbook, you are using numbers. What you are doing with them is adding and subtracting particular numbers to see if the amount of money you think you have is the same as the amount that the bank says you do. This is an empirical question with clear right and wrong answers.

Philosophy is not like that. Philosophers also think about numbers, but when they do, they don't worry about specific empirical questions like the right number of dollars in your bank account. They reflect on general, abstract questions about numbers themselves. Like the one I mentioned earlier: Since numbers are very different from the physical objects that we encounter during our everyday activities, can we say that they are equally real?

Or consider a young person who is thinking about whether to attempt to shoplift a candy bar. If she is thinking about whether she can get away with it, she is not thinking philosophically, but only calculating the likelihood of her success, an empirical question. But if she pauses and begins to reflect on whether stealing the candy would be wrong and why, then she is engaging in a philosophical inquiry, one that can't be solved simply by gathering information.

As this example illustrates, philosophy involves the attempt to justify judgments we make, such as, "Stealing is wrong." It involves specifying the criteria by means of which we make some fundamental distinctions that underlie many of our normal activities and judgments, such as that between right and wrong, but also true and false, real and imaginary, beautiful and ugly. Philosophers attempt to see what justification there is for making such distinctions. Sometimes they may find that there is none, and they then urge us to revise our ordinary ways of thinking and acting.

Philosophy includes very abstract theoretical questions, such as that about the nature of numbers, as well as questions that are more closely related to our everyday concerns, such as if, and why, stealing is wrong. There are philosophical questions that arise from puzzles encountered in every area of human endeavor. Philosophers, like young children, won't let go of those questions, but keep at them in hopes of coming up with an answer they and others will accept. Often times, though, those answers are not forthcoming; the best a philosopher can do is reject some inadequate ones, and that constitutes progress, too.

So even if philosophers can't tell you the right answers to all the questions that puzzle them and you, they can explain why many proposed answers are flawed. The important thing about philosophy, many philosophers believe, is the quest and not the final result.

Reading This Book

The bulk of this book consists of sixteen chapters, each of which highlights a particular picture book and a specific philosophical issue. You may read the chapters in any order, though they are arranged in a sequence. The first five chapters develop themes in metaphysics and the related fields of the philosophy of language and the philosophy of mind. All three are attempts to understand the nature of reality, although they take slightly different paths to uncover its nature. Although the explicit subjects of the following four chapters are knowledge, religion, logic, and art, they are all related in that they raise questions about the way that we think about the world. The final seven chapters of the book feature issues in ethics and social and political philosophy.

So, although there is a logical progression among the chapters, I have kept them pretty independent of one another. If you have a specific interest in philosophy, I suggest that you jump to the chapter that addresses that topic.

Throughout the book you will encounter the names of important philosophers (indicated in **bold type**). You'll find a brief biography of each in a special section at the back of the book. There, you will also find a glossary of key philosophical terms. Although all the terms I employ are explained in the book itself, the glossary lets you find one you are puzzled by quickly and easily. And in case you are interested in investigating the philosophical issues at the heart of other picture books, I have included an annotated list of some books that I would recommend taking a look at. Finally, you'll find a section listing different options for continuing your investigation of philosophy itself.

There are text boxes scattered throughout the book. Most of these introduce the philosophical field or issue discussed in the chapter in more depth. Feel free to skip these as you are reading the chapter. I have included them for those of you who are interested in learning about philosophy in a bit more depth.

I also want to call attention to the discussion suggestions at the end of each chapter. I thought you might be interested in some guidance if you were thinking about discussing the philosophical issue or issues raised by a book with a child or a group of children. Hopefully, you'll find my suggestions useful and a child might be just the person with whom you can have a fruitful discussion about a vexing philosophical issue. Children often can get you to see an issue in a refreshing, new light.

A final caveat: As you read this book, you may find yourself disagreeing with how I interpret one of the picture books that you know well. I was actually surprised to discover how difficult it is to accurately characterize the philosophical issue or issues raised by a book. But even when you disagree with me about what I say about a book, you'll be engaging philosophically with the book, which is, after all, the goal of this book.

Enough with the preliminaries. It's time to turn the page and start reading my account of how many of our most beloved children books actually bring us face to face with features of reality that don't make obvious sense, thereby launching us on the road to thinking – and to discussing – philosophy.

1

Harold and the Purple Crayon

Can You Get Wet Swimming in an Imaginary Ocean?

Can you get wet swimming in an imaginary ocean?

On the very first right-hand page of Crockett Johnson's *Harold and the Purple Crayon*, we see Harold, a young toddler, standing with his body facing to our left but with his head turned slightly to the right. He is looking behind himself with his eyes slightly raised and wearing one of those one-piece pajamas with booties for toddlers, a fact denoted by the single brownish line with which the picture of them is drawn. His hands and head are distinguished from the pajamas by being shaded a light gray. In his right hand, Harold holds his large and, as we shall see, very special purple crayon. At this point, Harold seems to have only scribbled with this crayon on a piece

A Sneetch Is a Sneetch and Other Philosophical Discoveries: Finding Wisdom in Children's Literature, First Edition. Thomas E. Wartenberg. Illustrations © Joy Kinigstein.
© 2013 John Wiley & Sons, Inc. Published 2013 by John Wiley & Sons, Inc.

of paper or, perhaps, a wall, making a large abstract drawing that we see depicted in the left-hand page of the book with a thickish purple line.

The reason Harold's head is cocked becomes clear when we read the accompanying text, for it says that it's now evening and Harold has decided to go for a moonlit walk. Harold's head is turned because he is looking for the moon, which unfortunately is nowhere in sight. How can he go on a moonlit walk if there is no moon? Our attempt to answer this question will require us to dive right into the most abstract of philosophy fields, *metaphysics*.

The book's next spread provides a first indication of what's unusual about Harold's crayon. From the text, we learn that Harold not only needs the moon to take his moonlit stroll, but also a path to walk on. The images convey something more significant, for Harold uses his purple crayon to make simple line drawings of these two objects.

Drawing the very objects he needs for his walk doesn't explain how Harold will be able to embark on his excursion. After all, if you want to go on a moonlit walk, just drawing pictures of the moon and a path in the margins of this book would not suffice. You need both the real moon and a real path for your walk. But in the fictional world created by *Harold and the Purple Crayon*, Harold's drawings suffice for his adventures. How can this be?

As we quickly learn, Harold's crayon has the special property of making drawings whose objects become real things. Your drawing of a path is just that, a drawing. And while you can walk all over it, when you do so, you won't be walking on a path but at most on a drawing of one. Your path exists only *as* a drawing or, to use the more general philosophical term, a *representation*.

A representation of an object is a sort of stand-in for that object. It denotes or refers to the real thing, but is not itself that object. For this reason, metaphysicians going all the way back to **Plato** treated representations as metaphysical second-class citizens. A representation of a bed is not real in the same way that an actual bed is.

Representations come in a variety of different forms. The most prolific are images. Drawings, paintings, digital images, even sculptures are representations when they have images that denote real things. Thus, the image of the path printed on the third spread of *Harold and the Purple Crayon* is a representation of a real path, something that might exist in the real world.

Metaphysics

Are the path and the moon that Harold has drawn real? What about the moon you see in the night sky? Or the inhabited ones in science fiction movies? And if the inhabited movie moons aren't real, as most people believe, how can we even perceive them? These are the sorts of puzzles that delight *metaphysicians*.

Metaphysics was traditionally the most basic area of philosophy, for its questions had to be resolved before questions in other areas could be tackled. Only once you knew what existed, could you wonder about questions of knowledge, conduct, or any of the other issues that puzzle philosophers.

One of the chief goals of metaphysics is to establish which things among the vast riches that populate our world are really real, have "first-class" being. Consider what philosophers call "the bent stick illusion." A straight stick like a pencil placed into a glass of water appears bent, but, once you withdraw it, it returns to its original shape. How can a stick do this?

The answer is that the stick merely *appeared* to bend in the water because of the difference between how water and air reflect light. The bent stick is thus placed into the category of less real things, for it is merely an *appearance* of the stick, which is itself fully real.

Beginning with **Plato**, philosophers have relegated all sorts of things to the realm of appearances, things that lack first-class reality. For Plato, everyday objects were not fully real, a theory known as *idealism*. The Roman philosopher-poet **Lucretius**' *materialist* viewpoint denied that minds were among the ultimate constituents of reality. Cartesian *dualism* (see **Descartes**) treats both minds and matter as equally basic, though it has the problem of explaining their interaction.

A related metaphysical distinction is between things that are real and things that are merely imaginary. While metaphysicians agree that unicorns and mermaids are less real than things that actually exist, such as the horses, fish, and people from which the elements of these imaginary things are derived, they puzzle over how things that don't exist can be thought about at all.

Of course, the image itself does exist as an object in our world just as a painting does. But the objects in Harold's drawing or in a painting are just representations, not the full-bloodied physical things that they represent.

This brief excursus into metaphysics gives us a better way to characterize Harold's world: The objects Harold draws don't only exist as representations, but acquire the first-class metaphysical citizenship that real things have. And that's why Harold is able to set off on a moonlit walk: When he makes a drawing, the objects he draws morph from mere representations into real things. So off he goes for his walk – carrying his purple crayon.

Harold's subsequent bedtime adventures all follow the same pattern. Initially, Harold is confronted by a problem, such as how to take a moonlit walk in the absence of the moon and a path on which to walk. He solves his problem by drawing a picture that contains the objects he needs, the moon and a path in this case. Because of the peculiar metaphysics of his world, these objects solve his problems when they morph from drawings into real things. But the reality of the morphed objects repeatedly confronts Harold with new problems: In this case, he does not know where he is going on the path he now stands upon. How can he keep from getting lost? So the cycle repeats itself as Harold draws his way to a new solution that presents a further problem, and so on.

One very amusing example of this pattern occurs when Harold draws a dragon. Previously, Harold had drawn a tree and worried that something would eat all the apples growing on it. Harold solves that problem with his dragon drawing. Resorting to a dragon for apple-guard-duty could only occur to a creative young child whose world is richly populated with such imaginary creatures. Harold's drawings put us in touch with his fecund imagination and are a source of enjoyment for us.

But Harold now has to face the fact that the apple-protecting dragon scares him. When Harold made his drawing of the dragon, he certainly didn't expect it to scare *him*. But once he sees his own creation – now morphed into a real dragon – he becomes so scared that his own shaking hand holding his beloved purple crayon inadvertently draws an ocean in which Harold almost drowns.

Harold's drawing of and subsequent encounter with a dragon illustrates the ingenuity with which Crockett Johnson, the book's author and illustrator, creates Harold's adventures. But these adventures are not merely a source of enjoyment for us as we follow their twists and turns. They also provide an entryway into the imaginary world Harold inhabits before bedtime.

Do we really enter into Harold's imagination when we see what happens with his drawings? Think about it. Harold really is in bed, trying to get to sleep. So off he goes on an imaginary journey. What's first? How about a moonlit walk? But there's no moon out and no path. No problem. All he has to do is to imagine them and himself in the sparse landscape created by his imaginings.

If this sounds plausible to you as a way of understanding the book, you'll probably also agree that the purple crayon is a very concrete stand-in for Harold's imagination. When we see Harold making a drawing with his purple crayon in an illustration by Crocker Johnson, we are witnessing the workings of Harold's imagination.

There are a number of interesting philosophical claims that the book presents about the nature of the imagination. The first is that the products of the imagination can become as real to us as the objects that we normally take to be real. Most of the time, when you imagine something – like what it would be like to have a million dollars – you are very aware that there is a difference between the reality of, say, the chair you are sitting in and the reality of those million dollars. Philosophers in the *empiricist tradition*, like **John Locke** and **David Hume**, attempted to characterize the difference by means of the intensity of our perception of the objects. The real objects that we perceive give us a more lively and vivacious perceptual experience than those we imagine, they held.

Harold and the Purple Crayon suggests a problem with that view. Even if we mostly imagine things with less intensity than we perceive them, that's not always the case. Harold's encounters with an ocean and a dragon appear to have the same intensity as his usual perceptual experiences. If that's right, then this thought experiment shows the inadequacy of the empiricist attempt to distinguish real things from imaginary ones on the basis of the intensity of our experience of them.

Now you might be thinking that only children experience imaginary things with that much intensity. While children might be able to take the products of their imaginations to be real things, we adults know the difference between reality and the imagination.

There are problems with this idea. Although children used to be thought of as not having a firm grasp on the distinction between real things and imaginary ones, recent research in cognitive science has shown this not to be true. Very young children know, for example, that the stuffed animal they are playing with is not real even as they conduct their imaginary play with it.

can students cite, etc.?

In addition, there are certain contexts in which we adults experience imaginary things as equally real. When you go to a movie, watch a play, or, even more intensely, play a computer game, your involvement sometimes becomes so complete that it seems to you that the things you are seeing (and hearing) are not merely representations but real things.

When this happens, the metaphysical distinction between real things and merely imaginary ones dissolves for you, just as it does for Harold, and it is as if things that are merely representations acquire full-blooded reality. Think about when you were watching a scary movie and found yourself scared by, say, a purely imaginary knife being plunged into what is only the image of an actor's body, not even really that of the character he is playing. Wasn't that knife real at that specific moment? (This is a topic we will discuss further in chapter 9, when we talk about the philosophy of art.)

Or think about what it's like to play a computer game. You are represented in the game world by an avatar, a computer image that stands for you. Your avatar moves through the imaginary world of the game and has to confront various obstacles that it/you must overcome. While you are absorbed in the game, you simply are your avatar and what happens to it happens to you, so the game world assumes the status of the real world for you at that moment.

Harold's world as depicted in the book is like what you experience while absorbed in watching a scary film or playing a computer game, only his entire world is created by his purple crayon. In the imaginary world of *Harold and the Purple Crayon*, the imaginary things he draws become real.

Although we often think of children on a sort of deficit model as lacking important skills and capacities that adults have, there are a number of ways in which children actually outstrip adults. One is the power of their imaginations. *Harold and the Purple Crayon* is a testament to the power of children's imaginations, their ability to give reality to things we adults can only dream about. Think of how a child talks to their favorite stuffed animal and holds it tight. When they do so, they are using their imaginations to make something real, as real as anything else in their world, something we adults normally lack the power to do.

Likewise, Harold inhabits the make-believe world created by his crayon so completely that he is able to interact with its objects. Or so Crockett Johnson's drawings – themselves drawn as if Harold had actually made them – show. When Harold is drowning in the ocean he accidentally drew, he really is immersed in it, both in Johnson's drawing and in Harold's imagination. Johnson depicts the contents of Harold's imagination so that we literally see him embedded among the objects he draws.

have students do this for hw

A somewhat different way of representing the world that children inhabit is used by Bill Watterson in his wonderful *Calvin and Hobbes* comics. In some strips, Watterson first draws panels that present the world that Calvin imagines, only to remove all the features due to Calvin's imagination in a later panel. What's so unique about *Harold and the Purple Crayon* is that we never see the world as it "really is," but only the world as structured by Harold's imagination.

There is only one incident in which the book shows us reality and not just Harold's imaginings. Harold is ready to go home so he can sleep. To find his room, Harold draws some windows, hoping to find the window of his bedroom. But no matter how many windows he draws – he ends up drawing a small city with skyscrapers – he can't find the right one. Suddenly he remembers something that distinguishes the window of his room from all the other windows he has seen: His window is always "right around the moon." Harold once again has the solution to his problem: he simply draws the moon inside a square that symbolizes a window, thus making that square become the window of *his* bedroom. Once he has encircled the moon in the square that is his window, Harold is suddenly located inside his room. This is because he has drawn the view he always sees from *inside* his room. So when he recreates that view with his purple crayon, Harold is transported from the world outside his house to the world inside his room.

This shows that the imagination not only has the power to depict objects that seem completely real to us, but also has the power to take us wherever we want to go. Even so, sometimes you can imagine that you are exactly where you really are.

And this is what happens to Harold in the final pages of the book. He imagines himself not only inside his room, but also actually in his bed. His final act is to *draw up* the covers of his bed – notice the pun on "drawing" here – and this allows him to go to sleep. When we see the final picture of Harold, he is asleep in his bed, but he has not drawn himself sleeping. He really is sleeping and we see that by his closed eyes, a feature of the world that he has not drawn. And this explains why Harold is himself depicted differently by Johnson than all the objects that Harold draws.

This brings us back to the question of whether there is a criterion that allows us to distinguish real objects from imaginary ones. Unlike Crockett Johnson's drawing, the world does not present imaginary objects to us in a distinctive style that provides us with a way to determine that they are products of the imagination, as we have just seen. Does this mean we are stuck in the skeptical position of not being able to say what makes an object real instead of imaginary?

Fortunately, I think not. **Immanuel Kant** proposed a different type of criterion that I think works well. Instead of relying on intrinsic differences between real objects and imaginary ones, Kant thought that real objects were simply those that cohered with other real objects to make up the world that we inhabit.

I think that Kant's account is correct. Most of the time, the objects you perceive – such as the page or screen on which you are reading this book – count as real because you fit them into a more general pattern with other objects you take to be real. You also know that the death of Marion Crane, the character played by Janet Leigh in *Psycho*, is not real because, when the film ends, her death doesn't fit with all the other events and things you take to be real, except when you take it to be something that happens in the film's imaginary world.

This is a *coherentist* account of the distinction between reality and the products of the imagination. The criterion it posits for judging an experience to be real is not based on any intrinsic quality of the experience, but on its connection to other experiences that also are real.

Before leaving *Harold and the Purple Crayon*, I feel compelled to discuss something that distinguishes it from most other picture books. It's no surprise, of course, that much of the charm of picture books comes from the wonderful drawings and illustrations that populate their pages. But delightful as they may be, a picture book's illustrations are not always necessary for understanding their stories. While we may love to look at the pictures in "Cookies," to choose the story I will discuss in chapter 12, we can understand the events that make up its story simply by paying attention to the words.

The pictures in *Harold and the Purple Crayon* play a more substantive role in our comprehension of the book's plot. The text alone does not fully communicate Harold's world to us. We only gain access to the imaginary world in which his bedtime adventures take place through the illustrations depicting his drawings, for they show us the world as he imagines it to be. Without them, the world of the story would be radically incomplete.

Thus, *Harold and the Purple Crayon* gives us an introduction to the metaphysical distinction between real and merely imaginary things, and even criticizes one attempt to develop an account of that distinction. It's time now to leave that distinction behind as we move on to the next chapter, where we'll concentrate on the metaphysical structure of those real things themselves.

Discussing Metaphysics with Children

Children love to think about the difference between real and imaginary things. Since the objects in Harold's drawings become real, consider beginning a discussion by asking them if they could have their hunger satisfied by eating drawings of pies, like Harold does. This can launch you into a discussion of what's peculiar about Harold's drawings and, hopefully, the difference between real things and imaginary ones. You might even ask whether they think Harold gets wet when he falls into the ocean he's drawn.

Good opening

Get Leon Lionni's
Let's Make Rabbits

2

The Important Book

Is a Leopard without Its Spots Still a Leopard?

Is a leopard without its spots still a leopard?

Margaret Wise Brown's *The Important Book* provides an excellent opportunity to continue the discussion of metaphysics we began in the last chapter. The book assumes that, of all the things true of any object, only one is *the important* thing about it. Using a sequence of different objects – a spoon, a daisy, rain, grass, snow, an apple, the wind, the sky, a shoe, and finally you – the book repeats a basic formula. On the two-page spread it devotes to each object, it first states what *the important thing* about that object is; then, it lists a number of *other things* that the object *also is*; finally, it repeats its designation of the important thing about the object.

In making a distinction between the important feature or property of an object and all the others that it simply is or has, *The Important Book* operates with the assumption that all objects have what metaphysicians call an *essential property*. As the book has it, while there are many things that are true of any object, only one is essential to it. These other things are *accidents* or non-essential properties of the object.

A Sneetch Is a Sneetch and Other Philosophical Discoveries: Finding Wisdom in Children's Literature, First Edition. Thomas E. Wartenberg. Illustrations © Joy Kinigstein.
© 2013 John Wiley & Sons, Inc. Published 2013 by John Wiley & Sons, Inc.

Essentialism

Essentialism is the metaphysical view that objects have one property – their *essential* property – that cannot change while the object remains the same thing. An object's other properties – its *accidents* – can change without altering the object's nature. Having a full head of hair and being bald are accidental properties of human beings. Having three sides is an essential property of triangles. You can be the same person you are, even if you lose all your hair, but a triangle that does not have three sides, say because you erase one of them, ceases to be a triangle.

    Aristotle first articulated the theory of essentialism. He was fascinated by the problem of change that had puzzled his predecessors, the **pre-Socratics**. What those philosophers could not understand was how a thing could change and yet still be the same thing. **Parmenides** and his followers, deciding that change was completely unintelligible, claimed that reality was completely unchanging. **Heraclitus** and his followers took the opposite horn of the dilemma, maintaining that things were always in a constant state of flux, and stating, "You cannot step into the same river twice for new waters are ever flowing."

    Aristotle took essentialism, in which a substance with an essential property is posited, to solve the problem of change. Subsequent philosophers have disagreed about the viability of Aristotle's metaphysics. It's easy to find the essential property of a mathematical entity like a triangle, because it has a specific, geometric definition: a three-sided plane figure. This definition specifies the essential properties of a triangle and all its other properties are non-essential or accidental.

    But with non-mathematical entities, formal definitions are not easy to come by. It's not at all clear, for example, how to define a desk or a chair in a way that allows one to see which properties of either object are essential. Desks may be things that you can write on, but not everything you can write on is a desk. And you can sit on desks as well as on chairs. So the usefulness of the distinction between essential and accidental properties of substances remains a contested issue within metaphysics.

*Good
exercise
for
students*

You'll get a better sense of what the book assumes if we focus on the book's discussion of one object. How about *rain*? After stating that the important thing about rain is that it is *wet*, the book declares that rain also falls from the sky, sounds like rain, makes things shiny, has no taste, and is the color of air. Finally, the first assertion – that the important thing about rain is that it is wet – is repeated.

I'm sure that you are puzzled by a number of the things the book says that rain is. Some seem true but uninformative, others completely false. Let's look at each statement in turn.

First, I don't think that rain is wet. Rain *makes things wet*, but that's different from *being wet*. The towel I left out in the rain is wet, but the rain . . . I think that it is neither wet nor not wet, i.e. dry. It's rain, after all, and rain makes things wet without being wet itself.

The statement that rain sounds like rain is either true but uninformative or false. On the one hand, it might be what philosophers call a *tautology*, something that we know to be true just using the laws of logic. (We'll discuss those more fully in chapter 8.) Everything sounds like itself, so rain does also. On the other hand, there might be no single sound that rain has, for how rain sounds depends on what it's falling *on*. Rain on a tin roof sounds very different than rain falling on a lake. So there really is no single sound that rain has.

The book is simply wrong when it claims that rain makes everything it falls on shiny. It makes some things shiny when it falls on them, like a paved road, but not others, like a newspaper, which it turns into a soggy mess.

Does it have no taste, as the book says? Probably that depends on the person tasting it. If I said that the rainwater tasted really refreshing, would I be saying that it had a taste?

In addition, air has no color; it's transparent. So how could rain have a non-existent color as its color?

Each of the claims the book makes about rain – for example, that it makes things shiny – is an empirical claim, that is, a claim about something factual. And we can disagree with what the book says in each case, as I have just done.

But the book's empirical mistakes don't entail that it is not making an interesting non-empirical, metaphysical claim about objects. Here is how I would put that claim: Each object has an important property, one that has a different status than all the object's other properties. So let's ponder what the book might have in mind when it says that there are many things that an object just is but only one special thing that is the important thing about it.

A first start would be to say that there are some things about any object that it doesn't necessarily have to be. Think about a leopard. Dictionary.com defines a leopard as "a large, spotted Asian or African carnivore, *Panthera pardus*, of the cat family, usually with tawny black markings." Basically, this boils down to saying that a leopard is a particular type of large spotted cat. So you might wonder if something could be a leopard and not have any spots. Although this may contradict the adequacy of the definition, the answer is yes, for there are albino leopards, leopards without spots. The question about the existence of leopards without spots is an empirical one. Facts about leopards determine what things are leopards.

Another feature of leopards posited by the definition is that they are members of the cat family. Here, we can ask a similar question: Could something be a leopard and not be a cat? This time, the answer is no. In order for something to be a leopard, it has to be a particular type of cat. If it isn't a type of cat, it just isn't a leopard.

The question of whether something could be a leopard and not be a cat has a non-empirical aspect to it. That's because our classificatory system requires anything that is a leopard is also a cat, for what leopards are is a specific species of cat. This doesn't mean that we might not some day discover that we were wrong about what leopards are, only that, given our current knowledge, leopards must be cats.

This example helps us understand *The Important Book*'s contrast of the thing that is important about an object and other things that it simply is. The thing that is *important* about an object is that which it has to have to be the object that it is and so could not lack: a type of cat in the case of a leopard. And things that an object *also is* are those things that the object could lack while still being the thing it is: spotted in our example of leopards.

As I suggested earlier, there is a bit of philosophical terminology that clarifies the issue, the distinction between essential and accidental properties. When *The Important Book* says that there is something important about an object, it is claiming that that feature is the object's essential property. All the other things about the object are its accidental properties, features that it just has, but that it could also lack.

Once again, an example might help make this clearer. Most of us have occasion to make ice cubes. We take an ice cube tray and fill it with water, put it into a freezer, and – lo and behold – ice emerges after a sufficient lapse of time. The water was clear and a liquid, but the ice usually has some white lines running through it and is a solid that shatters when hammered.

Where once there was a clear liquid, there is now a somewhat opaque and lined solid. How could this happen?

You likely can supply the answer. Underlying water and ice is the same substance, H_2O. Depending on the temperature, it will have different properties. Above 32 °F (0 °C), it is a clear liquid; below that, it becomes a slightly opaque solid. Even when its properties such as color and state change, the essential nature of H_2O remains the same. Only if a substance's chemical structure changed, would its nature change.

And this can happen. It is possible to pass an electric current through H_2O and to separate the hydrogen and the oxygen from each other. But when you do that, the nature of the substance would have undergone a change, a substantial change, and it would no longer be the type of thing it once was.

So even if it makes all sorts of empirical mistakes about the objects it talks about, *The Important Book* introduces us to a very important metaphysical schema, that involving substances that have both essential and accidental properties.

There is one question about the nature of this metaphysical schema that I would like to pose before ending my discussion of *The Important Book*. While discussing how water could become ice without no longer being the thing that it is, I slipped in the idea that water is actually H_2O. What I didn't call attention to was that fact that I had implicitly referred to the chemical composition of water and ice, the stuff both are made of. I used the fact that water and ice share the same chemical composition to explain why water can become ice and still be the same thing.

But think for a moment of a different object that *The Important Book* also analyzes: a spoon. A spoon does not have to be made out of specific physical constituents. There are metal spoons, wooden spoons, plastic spoons, even paper ones. Does this mean that spoons are a counter-example to the claim that all things have an essential property, that is, an example of something that does not have an essential property?

Not at all. The important thing about a spoon is that it is an implement that can hold liquids. (That might not distinguish a spoon from a cup or a ladle, but let's ignore those complications for the purposes of this discussion.) So rather than being made *out of* particular stuff – as water and ice are – spoons are things that are used *for* a specific *purpose*.

This shows that we classify things on the basis of different features. Some we take to be essentially made of a particular type of matter; others we

Counterexamples

Philosophers love to define things, from knowledge to goodness. They put forward definitions like "knowledge is justified true belief" and "an action is right if it contributes the most to human welfare." These are general claims and one way to think about whether they are accurate is to try to come up with examples that don't fit the definition. So if you can think of an example of justified true belief that is not knowledge or an act that is moral but that doesn't contribute the most to the general welfare, then you have come up with a counterexample to that definition of knowledge or morality.

Taking a look at an actual philosophical counterexample will help us understand this important tool in the philosopher's repertoire. In the opening sections of *The Republic*, **Plato** presents a clear counterexample to a proposed definition of justice. One of the participants in the conversation in which **Socrates**, Plato's mouthpiece, is taking part proposes the following definition of justice: Giving back to people what they are owed.

Socrates' counterexample to this proposed definition involves a short narrative. Suppose, he says, that you borrowed a weapon from someone but that person has gone mad and comes to you asking for it back. You know that he is mad and realize that he will be a danger to himself and others if you give him back his weapon. So it's clear what the right or just thing to do is, namely, refusing to return the weapon to the person whose weapon it is. But that contradicts the proposed definition of justice and is, thus, a counterexample to it.

Counterexamples are an important tool of the philosopher. They help refine our knowledge by showing us inadequacies in our beliefs.

conceive as necessarily serving certain functions. Natural things – such as water and ice (as well as leopards) – are generally regarded as having a specific physical structure – H_2O, in the case of water. But spoons, glasses, and other artifacts (things created by us) are identified by the function they serve. That's why a spoon is a "for-slurping-liquids" thing. Sometimes we use a *structural* characterization to classify things, other times a *functional* one.

If you now look at what *The Important Book* claims are the important things about the objects is describes, you may be surprised. Here is the list:

Object	The Important Thing About
A spoon	You eat with it
A daisy	It is white
Rain	It is wet
Grass	It is green
Snow	It is white
An apple	It is round
The wind	That it blows
The sky	It is always there
A shoe	You put your foot in it
You	You are you

A quick perusal of this chart reveals that *The Important Book* does not have a uniform metaphysical view about the nature of objects in our world. In the case of a spoon, it gives a functional characterization of it, but in all the other cases it does not. Sometimes, as in the case of a daisy, grass, and an apple, the book treats physical properties as the essential ones, e.g. having a certain color or shape. With other objects, it's just not clear what type of property the book has in mind, as when it says that the important thing about the sky is that it is always there.

So even though the book employs a substance-property metaphysical schema in its presentation of a number of different objects, it does not have a consistent understanding of the nature of the substances it describes. But, probably, that's not all that surprising. *The Important Book* is not, after all, a philosophical treatise but a children's picture book. It's impressive that it has opened up for our reflection the viability of a certain metaphysical account of the nature of objects. It's up to you – and a favorite child, perhaps – to pursue this philosophical issue further and more consistently than the book has.

Discussing Essentialism with Children

The Important Book presents an area of metaphysical investigation that it's easy to discuss with children. You can take any of the objects the book

opening
Exersize
/ for
the
class

discusses, from a spoon to rain, and ask the children to tell you all the things they think are true of that object. Once you have developed a list, you can then ask if there is one thing that is the *important* thing about that object, something that it has to be to be that very object. It's also useful to compare the book's list with theirs, asking which they think is better and why.

A more advanced discussion would involve looking at a list of objects and their important things similar to the one presented in the chart printed above. The issue you could ask about is what makes the important thing for that object *the* important thing about it. You would be thinking about the different types of important things (i.e. essential properties) that objects have in order to see what basis there is for the distinction between things an object simply is and those things that are important about it.

3

Shrek!

Could a Dead Skunk Smell Good?

Could a dead skunk smell good?

The world of William Steig's perverse yet charming fairytale, *Shrek!*, is a topsy-turvy one. Shrek, the ugliest being imaginable, is pretty much the opposite of everything we think is good and valuable. He smells so bad that flowers and trees shrink from him. The hideous witch he meets seems lovely to him and her rank potions, just delicious. He pays her with lice for telling his fortune, and is delighted to find out that his bride-to-be is a princess even uglier than he. The peasant he meets on his quest faints from a mere glance at Shrek. Indeed, all creatures great and small run from him in horror. And yet Shrek is happy being who he is, seemingly content with the effect he has on everything around him.

What's more, Shrek is not scared by things that we tend to fear: lightning doesn't bother him and even a dragon cannot unnerve him, for Shrek breathes fire and belches smoke. What does scare this unusual creature are things that we find pleasurable: When he wakes from a dream in which a group of children are hugging and kissing him, for example, Shrek is relieved to realize that it was only a nightmare.

Even though you might expect Shrek to be unhappy that he is so ugly, smelly, and generally repulsive, he isn't. When he enters a hall of mirrors

A Sneetch Is a Sneetch and Other Philosophical Discoveries: Finding Wisdom in Children's Literature, First Edition. Thomas E. Wartenberg. Illustrations © Joy Kinigstein.

on his quest to find his beloved princess, Shrek sees hundreds of replicas of himself. Seeing how ugly each of them is, Shrek is not disgusted, as we might be, but thrilled to realize that all those ugly creatures are nothing but himself.

When he finally meets the princess of his dreams, Shrek is completely overwhelmed by her ugliness, just the way most of us would be by a person's beauty or handsomeness. The two fall madly in love, exchanging love poems in which they compare one another to disgusting things. And – you probably could have guessed this – they lived *horribly* ever after.

Like *The Important Book*, *Shrek!* raises a concern about the properties of objects. But *Shrek!* focuses on an issue in the *philosophy of language*, a relatively new area of philosophical investigation that first emerged during the twentieth century.

The Philosophy of Language

The philosophy of language takes the way we speak to be the primary topic for philosophical investigation. Buoyed by developments in logic (see chapter 8), philosophers saw language as having a logical structure that had remained hidden from previous investigators. Philosophers began to see every philosophical problem as rooted in the way in which language was used or misused.

An early group of philosophers who were interested in how illicit uses of language gave rise to philosophical problems were the *logical positivists*. Their theory of linguistic meaning stated that a word only had meaning if there were practical consequences that could be traced to its use. Armed with this theory, they attempted to show that many traditional problems could simply be dissolved by showing that they involved meaningless concepts.

The careful attention that philosophers of language paid to language itself brought about a philosophical style of writing that put a premium on precision and exactitude of meaning. *Analytic philosophy* remains the dominant form of philosophy in the English-speaking world and has had an impact on philosophy worldwide.

It will take a bit of explanation to describe the precise philosophical issue raised by *Shrek!* We can begin by noticing that Shrek's reaction to ugliness is pretty much the opposite of ours. Not only is Shrek pleased to see just how ugly he himself is, but he is excited to discover that his bride-to-be is even uglier and that's why he falls in love with her.

When you read that Shrek is attracted by his future spouse's ugliness, you are likely both surprised, amused, and a slight bit puzzled. There certainly is something very odd about being attracted to something that's ugly. Generally, ugly things repulse or disgust us. So it's a surprise to find Shrek pleased by the ugliness of his wife-to-be. Of course, such oddities are responsible for a great deal of our amusement in reading *Shrek!* But what makes us find them so *odd*?

To begin answering this question, let's consider at a very simple sentence: "That stinks!" This sentence has two distinct aspects to it. The obvious one is that it expresses your negative *evaluation* of something. When you say that something stinks, you are expressing your revulsion, a very strong negative reaction to it.

Your revulsion could be equally well expressed if you just said, "Yuck!" But "That stinks!" conveys an important, additional piece of information about your revulsion, namely, that it is the object's *smell* that revolts you. This component of the sentence is *descriptive*, for it tells you something about the world and not just about your feelings. So an expression like "That stinks!" has both an evaluative and a descriptive element to it. It says you are smelling something (descriptive), and that you don't like what you smell (evaluative).

Although we can distinguish the descriptive component of your statement from its evaluative one, as I have just done, we can also ask whether the two are actually distinct from each other. Can you really think of the smell of something completely disgusting – say the smell of a dead skunk – and imagine that you could find that very smell pleasant or enjoyable?

I think that many of you probably would deny that you could imagine finding a really disgusting smell pleasant under any circumstances. If you doubt this, think about using dead skunk as your next perfume or cologne. I think it's just not possible for you to imagine finding that very smell pleasurable, and many of you will probably shudder at the thought of *Moldy Dead Skunk* as the scent of your next cologne or after-shave. The smell of a dead skunk is just a completely disgusting smell, and there's no way to imagine that you might find it pleasant even if things were somehow differently constituted.

Now if you think that's right, then you are denying that, in regard to smells, the descriptive and evaluative aspects of language can be separated. This point can be generalized to hold for all the sensations that we have, those features of our experience that are most immediate and sensory. If you have ever tasted spoiled milk, you know that it tastes really horrible. You probably can't imagine finding such a taste pleasant. With each and every one of our immediate sensory experiences, our affective reactions – pleasure, pain, disgust, etc. – seem inherently connected to what we sense. Rotten milk just tastes *bad* and chocolate simply tastes *good*. We can't imagine our reactions being reversed.

You may be surprised to learn that some philosophers disagree with the claim that you cannot separate the descriptive and evaluative elements of linguistic statements. This is because they take descriptive statements to be the basic elements of language, to which our subjective attitudes get attached later in a contingent manner.

Ludwig Wittgenstein

Ludwig Wittgenstein was a charismatic figure who had a significant impact on the history of twentieth-century philosophy. He came from a rich Jewish family in Vienna, but he renounced his inheritance and lived a simple life. He went to Cambridge as a young man to study with another giant of twentieth-century philosophy, **Bertrand Russell**. The brilliant Russell was completely cowed by Wittgenstein's genius.

One reason Russell was so impressed by Wittgenstein is that Wittgenstein turned in a PhD dissertation which is now recognized as one of the great philosophical works of the twentieth century, his *Tractatus Logico-Philosophicus*. While most PhD dissertations sit on the shelves of libraries gathering dust, Wittgenstein's had an immediate impact. In part, this was because he developed a theory of language that gave pride of place to its descriptive aspect. He called his theory *the picture theory of language*. It asserted that the most basic function of language is to give us a picture of the world.

One of the interesting features of Wittgenstein as a philosopher was that he was not reluctant to say that he had changed his mind. By the time he wrote his second important book, *The Philosophical Investigations*, he had rejected his own earlier view. In its place, he developed an account of language that emphasized the role that language played in human activities. We will look more closely at this type of account of language in the next chapter.

Philosophers have proposed different answers to the question of whether language has a single basic function. Among the answers that have been proposed are: communicating, expressing, and picturing.

To see what distinguishes these theories from one another, think about our human ancestors. Why might they have begun to use language? The *communicative* theory of language points out that language has a beneficial effect on the survival of human beings because it allows them to communicate. When you notice a saber-toothed tiger about to attack your friend, you can scream, "Look out!", and thereby warn him.

The *expressive* theory of language emphasizes that language is used to express feelings. When you hit your thumb instead of a nail with a hammer, your yelling "Ouch!" expresses the pain you feel, just as shaking your hand and crying does.

The *picture* theory of language takes description to be language's basic function, providing a type of map of the world. In fact, this theory assumes that language is very much like a map, with words standing for things, just as a small image of a tree on a map might stand for a state park.

Take a sentence like the philosopher's stereotypical, "The cat is on the mat." The two most important parts of the sentence are its nouns, "the cat" and "the mat." Each refers to an object, the cat and the mat. The verb phrase "is on" actually obscures how language functions. It conveys the relationship between the cat and the mat, namely, that the cat is positioned above – or on – the mat. A more perspicuous language might simply contain the two nouns "the cat" and "the mat" in a specific physical configuration to picture the relationship "is on." In such a language, we might find the following representation of the fact that the cat is on the mat:

---

the cat

the mat

The picture theory claims that all other uses of language – communicative and evaluative included – supplement this basic picturing function.

What the picture theory enables a philosopher to claim is that the descriptive aspect of language is fundamental, with all others, including the evaluative one, added on later, as a sort of supplement. At its most basic level language presents a symbolic picture of facts in the world.

Of course, the evaluative function of language, its ability to convey our attitudes about things, is important. But Wittgenstein thought that this function of language was not its most basic one, at least at the time he wrote the *Tractatus*.

So who is right about the relationship between the descriptive and evaluative aspects of language, we – who can't imagine a dead skunk smelling good – or Wittgenstein – who thought that the purely descriptive part of language could be separated off from its less basic evaluative parts? And how would you go about showing that one view was the correct one?

That's where *Shrek!* comes in. It presents what philosophers call a *thought experiment*. A thought experiment is similar to a real experiment, except that you conduct it in your mind rather than in the real world.

Think back to when you were in high school. Maybe you took a physics course and had to perform an experiment to show how the speed of a car down an inclined plane varies over time. This was an *actual experiment* because you created a situation in which you could try to verify the scientific law that states that the speed of a falling object is proportional to the time it has fallen, to test the "law of falling bodies." You collected your data and saw whether the experiment confirmed or disconfirmed what the law states.

A *thought experiment* is similar to a physics experiment with the significant difference that it is performed in your head. In order to make a philosophical point, a philosopher will very often say something like this: "Imagine that you are having all the sense experience that you are now having, but there are no physical objects at all. Instead . . . " The idea is to fully imagine this hypothetical situation and then see if what the philosopher says you will think about it matches what you actually do think.

So the philosopher might continue, and here I'm reproducing an argument of **René Descartes**'s: there is one belief – that you exist – that would be true even if you were completely deceived about the existence of physical things. The thought experiment is supposed to confirm a certain philosophical theory – here, that your belief in your own existence cannot be doubted and hence that belief must be true (for if you doubt you exist, you must exist; otherwise there would be no one to do the doubting). In a philosophical thought experiment, once you have imagined the situation described, you are asked to acknowledge the philosopher's claim.

Thought experiments can be found in every field of philosophy, not just the philosophy of language and theory of knowledge. Ethics, for example, redounds with thought experiments such as the very famous trolley one. In it, you are to imagine a trolley barreling down a track out of control. There is a switch and you can throw it, causing the train to go down a different track. If you do nothing, the 10 people sitting on the track will be killed, but if you throw it, only one person will die. What should you do? This thought experiment has been alleged to show problems with the ethical theory of utilitarianism (see chapter 10).

The contemporary philosopher and art critic **Arthur Danto** used a whole raft of thought experiments to support his theory of art. Consider, for example, Robert Rauschenberg's *Bed*, a sort of hanging sculpture that includes a pillow, quilt, and sheet and looks more or less like a bed upon which paint has been spilled. What sort of mistake, Danto asks, would a person make if he took *Bed* off the wall and tried to sleep in it? Danto's answer – he would have mistaken a work of art for a bed – is intended to support his claims about the nature of works of art, namely that there are no visual properties that distinguish them for real things. (We'll discuss this and related issues in chapter 9.)

You actually have already conducted a philosophical thought experiment in thinking about the connection between your evaluative reactions to such immediate perceptions as smells and the descriptive contents of the sentences you use to report them. I asked you to imagine that you could find a disgusting smell pleasant. When you tried and then thought about whether you agreed with my claim that you couldn't, you were conducting a philosophical thought experiment.

If this thought experiment were definitive then it would show that Wittgenstein's views about language did not accurately describe at least some uses of language, namely those in which we reported how we experience tastes, smells, sounds, etc. But does this short thought experiment provide us with good grounds for rejecting that view?

Not if we are taken with the smelly ogre Shrek. For *Shrek!* presents a philosophical thought experiment that purports to show that the descriptive and evaluative contents of sentences are really distinct. It does this by describing in words and showing, in Steig's wonderful drawings, a creature – Shrek – whose visceral reactions to many things are the exact opposite of ours. He finds ugly things beautiful, likes things that we find repulsive. He also dislikes experiences that we enjoy, such as being hugged by little children. *Shrek!* is the embodiment of a thought experiment in which our standard evaluations of beauty and ugliness are reversed in the attitudes and reactions of Shrek.

If *Shrek!* portrays a creature who might possibly exist while acting and talking the way that he does, then we have to concede that the evaluative aspects of our statements are separable from their descriptive ones. As we have seen, Shrek's evaluative responses to things we find repulsive are the opposite of ours. If his responses are at least intelligible, it must be because the descriptive component of a claim like "She is the ugliest being alive" is separable from that which expresses one's reaction to that fact, namely that we find her repulsive.

What's particularly interesting about *Shrek!*, from a philosophical point of view, is that it cuts against our intuitions in regard to cases like that of the smell of a dead skunk. While it may well be impossible for us to really imagine that the very smell given off by a dead skunk could be anything other than disgusting, *Shrek!* suggests that this is just due to our parochialism, our mistake of taking our own experience of the world to be a suitable guide for judging how the world actually is.

We can garner some additional support for the validity of *Shrek!*'s philosophical point by considering vultures and other scavengers. As you've probably noticed while driving down a highway, these animals eat dead animals like skunks. And it makes sense to think that they must enjoy the smell and taste of the meat they eat. They certainly can't be disgusted by it, for they eat it with what can only be described as relish. Such scavengers resemble Shrek in that they appear to have the inverse of our association to the smell of dead skunk. And, if this is so, then there seems to be no inherent connection between the actual smell and the disgust that we experience when we smell it.

Even more support can be found in our own experience with, say, a "stinky" cheese that we initially find completely disgusting because of its smell. I remember being completely revolted when my father first introduced me to Limburger cheese, what I thought must have be the worst smelling cheese in the world. Its smell reminded me of the smell of socks that had been worn way too long. But after tasting the cheese and seeing how incredibly delicious it tasted, I changed my opinion about how Limburger cheese smelled. Although I still don't think it smells wonderful, I no longer find its smell nauseating, perhaps because I anticipate the pleasure I will feel when I taste it. And if you're not a fan of smelly cheeses, then what about foods whose sliminess bothered you before you came to love eating them in sushi? And while almost any child I know thinks that beer tasted awful the first time she tried it, that perception doesn't last long. "Hmmm," she comes to remark, "that doesn't really taste half bad."

A consequence of this series of reflections on *Shrek!* is that we should be wary of putting too much weight on our own intuitions in thinking about the world. *Shrek!* shows us that the structure of the world might not really match our intuitive sense of what it *must* be like. Even if we can't imagine a world in which rotten things smell good, there is no reason to believe that we are correct when we base our beliefs upon quickly formed intuitions about how things must be.

Through its topsy-turvy, inverted world, then, *Shrek!* not only gets us to see that the very way in which we describe the world conveys our attitude about it, but it gets us to see that our experience of the world, and hence our affective response to it, might have been very different. Language is not just a way to describe the things that compose our world; it is also a way to register our feelings about and attitudes towards them.

In getting us to accept this view of language, *Shrek!* is a great example of what I call "picture book philosophy." A great deal of the enjoyment we get out of reading this book involves our appreciating the oddity of the inverted world it creates in which the standard connection between facts and their appraisals is inverted. But the delight we feel as we read the book has a "serious" aspect to it, for, as I have been arguing, the inversions registered in *Shrek!* bring to the fore an aspect of language – its conveying of attitudes – that philosophers and ordinary people have often overlooked.

So *Shrek!*, like all the picture books I discuss in this book, can be an occasion for some very engaging philosophical reflection. William Steig has created a book that not only is enjoyable to read, but pushes us to reflect on the extent to which our experience of the world is an accurate guide to understanding its structure. And in so doing, it pushes us to think philosophically.

Discussing the Philosophy of Language with Children

You might start by asking a child what his or her favorite and least favorite foods are. You would follow up by asking whether they could imagine enjoying the taste of their least favorite food as much as they do that of their favorite one. If they say no, then ask them whether they think that Shrek would love the taste of their least favorite food and be disgusted by the taste of their favorite one? This would hopefully lead into a discussion of the relationship between tastes (and smells and looks) and our reactions to them.

4

Let's Do Nothing!

Can You Just Do Nothing at All?

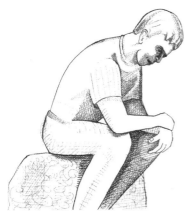

Can you just do nothing at all?

One day Sal and his friend Frankie, the protagonists of Tony Fucile's amusing book, *Let's Do Nothing!*, have done absolutely everything they can think of doing. They have played every sport they know how to play; they have painted and baked; they have played board games; they have even read comic books. Now they are bored. There is nothing left for them to do.

As Sal thinks about it, he realizes that's actually the solution, not the problem. They can do *nothing*. If that's all that's left for them to do, then why not just do it?

Although Sal thinks that he has solved his and Frankie's problem about what to do next, he's actually immersed them in a philosophical problem: *Is it possible to do nothing?*

To understand exactly what Sal and Frankie have stumbled into, consider what doing nothing would require. First of all, you couldn't move. But wait. If you're not moving, you probably are sitting or standing still, and

A Sneetch Is a Sneetch and Other Philosophical Discoveries: Finding Wisdom in Children's Literature, First Edition. Thomas E. Wartenberg. Illustrations © Joy Kinigstein.
© 2013 John Wiley & Sons, Inc. Published 2013 by John Wiley & Sons, Inc.

then you are still doing that and so, not doing nothing. You could lie down and hold your breath, but that doesn't solve the problem either. You are still doing something and, hence, not doing nothing.

So, is it really possible to do absolutely nothing at all? This question straddles the boundary between metaphysics and the philosophy of language, for the concept of nothing has been a very puzzling one to philosophers. But before entering those murky waters, let's see how Sal and Frankie fare in their attempt to do nothing.

Sal's initial idea about how to go about doing nothing is similar to the ones I've just described. What he and Frankie have to do in order to do nothing, he explains, is not move at all. So he suggests they pretend to be stone statues, for stone statues certainly don't move or do much of anything.

After only a short time, however, Frankie finds that he has trouble not moving. As he imagines himself a stone statue, he also imagines pigeons landing on him and doing you know what. So he tries to shoo them away and, in so doing, moves. But once he does that, he's definitely not doing nothing any more.

Their next attempt to do nothing, by pretending to be a couple of giant redwood trees, fares no better. This time Frankie, imagining himself to be an unmoving tree, moves to avoid being peed on by an imaginary dog. And so it goes. Every time that Sal suggests that they imagine themselves to be a different stationary object, Frankie moves because he imagines something bad happening to him while he's pretending to be that unmoving object. And once he moves, it's clear that he is no longer doing nothing.

After a brief bout of frustration with Frankie, Sal claims he's made an important discovery: *You can't do nothing.* Each time he and Frankie tried to do nothing, they failed not because of some fault of their own or because they didn't try hard enough. No, their attempt to do nothing *had* to end in failure. Nothing is simply not something you can do. Or so Sal claims. Frankie agrees, and the two of them head off to play once more, no longer obliged to try to do nothing.

But are they right? Can you really not do nothing?

Sometimes, we do claim to be doing nothing. Say that you are wrapping a birthday present for your son and he inadvertently comes into the room. You quickly throw the present and the wrapping paper into a drawer, open your computer, and look at the screen, pretending to be absorbed by what you see on it. When your son asks you "What are you doing?", you reply, "Oh, nothing," in order not to tell him what you are actually doing, for that would ruin the surprise. Imagine saying this instead: "I'm just sitting here on the computer, pretending to be occupied, because I don't want you to know that I've just thrown your present into a drawer so that you won't know that I was wrapping it." That's *actually* what you were doing, and that's precisely what you are trying to conceal from your son so that he will be surprised by his birthday present. So you when you say that you are doing nothing, you are not really claiming that what you are doing is *nothing*. Rather, you are *saying* that you are doing nothing in order to prevent your son from finding out what you are really doing.

Deceiving your son this way is an example of a white lie, a topic in ethics whose morality we will discuss in more detail in chapter 10. What matters here is that because you are being deceptive, we can't take your sentence's literal meaning – according to which *nothing* is what you are doing – to be what is conveyed to your son by your saying that you are doing nothing.

Ordinary Language Philosophy

Ordinary language philosophy is less a field of philosophy than an approach to dealing with philosophical issues. It is a specific stance in the philosophy of language, one that rejects the attempt to treat our common ways of speaking as based on a concealed logical structure. In place of that, it substitutes careful attention to the way in which language is ordinarily used. Ordinary language philosophers thought that, if you paid sufficient attention to how words are actually used, philosophical problems could be dissolved.

Consider, for example, the claim that we can only have knowledge if we know some things with absolutely certainty. The philosopher **René Descartes**, whom we encountered in the last chapter, used this claim to undermine our faith in sense perception, because sometimes we make mistakes about what we see. But ordinary language philosophers claim that Descartes's use of the word "certainty" is idiosyncratic, that there are many beliefs that are derived from sense perception that we can be certain of, in fact, as certain of as we are of anything else.

Ludwig Wittgenstein and **J.L. Austin** are two of the most important proponents of the ordinary language approach to the philosophy of language. Each had a large impact upon future generations of philosophers.

It is important for you to notice that my discussion has proceeded by paying careful attention to the actual way in which the phrase "I am doing nothing" might be used. This attention to how language is actually used by people is characteristic of a particular approach to the philosophy of language known as *ordinary language philosophy*.

So this example of saying that you are doing nothing doesn't really answer Sal and Frankie's question, "Can you do nothing?" When you say you are doing nothing, you are just dodging the question, not actually saying that you are engaged in the specific activity of *doing nothing*. So maybe Sal and Frankie are right to claim that you can't do nothing. If, whenever we *say* we are doing nothing, we don't really *mean* that we are doing nothing, maybe we can't really just *do* nothing at all. The reason it appears that we're doing nothing is because that is what we say we're doing, but our words don't mean what they literally say.

But haven't we just jumped from the frying pan into the fire? In order to explain why we can't do nothing, we claimed that what our words say is not what we really mean. How are we going to explain *that*?

Fortunately, I've got a card up my sleeve to resolve this worry. All we need to do is make a distinction between a sentence and a statement. A *sentence* is something that is composed of words. The sentence "I am doing nothing" is composed of four words, namely, "I," "am," "doing," and "nothing." The sentence can be written down, as I have done, or it can be spoken. The words that make up the sentence also can be written down or spoken, but they are nonetheless distinct words.

A sentence has a meaning, which is a composite of the meaning of the words that compose it. The meaning of the sentence, "The sky is blue," is a function of the meaning of its parts: "the," "sky," "is," and "blue." *The sky* is the object that we generally see when we look up and *blue* is a specific color. The *is* – philosophers refer to this as "the copula" – connects the two other parts of the sentence into a meaningful whole.

We utter sentences in order to make *statements*. A statement is the meaning that a person conveys to another when she uses a sentence in a specific situation. The most basic relationship between a sentence and a statement is when a sentence is used to make a statement whose meaning is simply that of the sentence itself. As I've already mentioned, philosophers seem to love the sentence, "The cat is on the mat," for reasons I don't understand. In any case, in the last chapter, while discussing the picture theory of language, we saw how the various words in the sentence contributed to its overall meaning.

What statement does the sentence, "The cat is on the mat," express? It states that the cat is on the mat. You might utter this sentence in response to, say, a family member asking you where the cat is. When you answer, "The cat is on the mat," you are providing a piece of information that locates the cat for your family member. She might be on the floor or outside, but, no, she's on the mat.

But not all statements have meanings that are identical with the meanings of the sentences that are used to make them. An example will bring this home.

We're all familiar with sarcasm. Often, a person makes a sarcastic remark by using a word or sentence but marking it as sarcastic by giving the saying of it a specific inflection. Consider the meaning of my response, "Great!", to my son's informing me that he has had a car accident. What I'm clearly *not* doing is telling my son that I think it's really wonderful that he has been in a car accident, though that's what my utterance literally says. The tone of voice and context for my saying, "Great!", makes it clear that I really intend to express more or less the opposite of what the sentence literally says, that I think it's very unfortunate he was in a car accident.

So a person can use a word or a sentence to make a statement whose meaning is not the literal meaning of the word(s) she utters. Generally speaking, the meaning of a statement is the result of a transformation of the meaning of the sentence used to make it. In my response to my son, the statement I made means pretty much the opposite of what the sentence says. My sarcastic tone of voice is a verbal marker that inverts the meaning of what I literally said.

Here's another example that will help us solve our problem of doing nothing. Say that your daughter walks into a room where you are half-heartedly watching a football game on TV. "What are you doing?" she asks, although she can, you may think, see that pretty clearly for herself. But she's not really asking you to tell her what you're doing. She's issuing you an invitation to do something with her. If you are not really interested in the game, you likely would reply, "Nothing," or "I'm doing nothing." As in our earlier example, when you say this, the statement you intend to convey to her is that she wouldn't be interrupting you if she wanted to do something with you or ask you something, and that you're quite willing to do or talk about whatever she wants. But that is not what your words literally mean.

So it would be very odd if she replied, "Great! Let's do nothing together!", much in the vein of Sal and Frankie's abortive project. Such an odd reply would indicate that she didn't really understand what you were trying to say, what statement you intended to make. If she did say that to you, it would be much more likely either that she didn't understand what you meant to convey or else that she was being sarcastic, making some type of statement about how she thought your interest in football was a complete waste of time.

Distinguishing between the meaning of a sentence and a statement allows us to see that generally, when we say we are doing nothing, that's not literally what we mean, although that is the meaning of the words that we utter. We are using that sentence to make a very different statement whose meaning depends on the context in which we utter the sentence.

In general, then, when we *say* that we are doing nothing, we don't *literally mean* that. While this provides some support to Sal's contention that you can't do nothing, it doesn't fully justify it, but only undermines the grounds for denying its truth. To develop positive support for his claim, we'll need to take another foray into the philosophy of language.

When Sal and Frankie attempted to do nothing, they were misled by the phrase "do nothing." "I am doing nothing" has the structure of a pronoun–verb–object sentence in which:

I = pronoun
am doing = verb
nothing = object

But philosophers of language in the early part of the twentieth century, who we encountered in the last chapter, taught us that we need to be suspicious of what they called "the surface grammar" of a sentence. The real grammar of a sentence, its *deep structure*, is the one that determines its meaning and often differs from the one specified by grammar books. In this case, "nothing" is really the first component of the sentence and it says that "There is no [activity]." The rest of the sentence has to be construed like this: "I am doing it."

To see the validity of this analysis, consider a slightly simpler sentence: "I ate nothing." You might respond in this way to someone's question about how the food was at a restaurant they saw you leaving. (You may only have had a cup of coffee or a martini.) What you are not saying is that nothing is the thing that you ate. If you ate an apple, you would, of course, say, "I ate an apple." The problem is that the sentence, "I ate nothing" has a different deep structure than the sentence, "I ate an apple," even though they share the same surface grammar.

So what are you saying when you say, "I ate nothing"? Something like this:

There is no [food], such that I ate it.

As in our earlier statement, the phrase "there is no . . ." functions as a denial of a sentence, here "I ate it." It says that no matter what you put in the place of the "it" – "an apple," "a steak," "dinner" – you won't get a true statement.

So if Sal and Frankie tried to play the game "Let's eat nothing," they wouldn't be trying to eat a new type of food called "nothing." Their aim would be to refrain from eating any food whatsoever. Although this would probably not be a very interesting game to play for very long, our analysis of the deep structure of the game's title shows us that they are not engaged in the quixotic attempt to eat something called "nothing."

I haven't yet explained the presence of brackets in my reformulation of "I ate nothing." The presence of the brackets is to demonstrate that there is an implicit range of things that you can substitute for the "it" in "I ate it," usually foods, although in exceptional cases other things. (Imagine responding to a doctor worried that you swallowed a nail, "but I ate nothing!")

This helps explain how Sal and Frankie got themselves into trouble by trying *to do nothing*. "Let's do nothing" is a type of self-defeating sentence. When you say to someone, "Let's . . ." you are inviting them to join you in some type of activity. "Let's go to the movies" and "Let's take a walk" are two simple examples of activities you might invite someone to engage in with you by saying, "Let's . . ." So what you need to know, when someone says "Let's . . ." is what activity they are inviting you to engage in.

The problem with "Let's do nothing" is that it is an invitation to engage in the activity of *doing nothing*. But, as we just saw, "nothing" is not the name of some vacuous thing but rather a denial, in this case, of any particular activity. So the two parts of the sentences contradict one another. You are saying:

(i)   Let's engage in the activity of . . .
(ii)   Not engaging in any activity.

And the reason that doesn't make sense is that (ii) is not something you engage in at all.

Here's an analogy that may clarify this point. Say that we are playing the children's game in which one person hides something in her hand and the other has to guess what it is. It's my turn and I have something in my hand, so you have to guess what it is. You try. A coin. Nope. A pebble. Nope. A bottle cap. Once more, nope. No matter what you guess, I tell you that you are wrong, it's not what you guessed.

Frustrated, you give up and ask me what I had concealed in my fist. My response is, "Oh, just something." You would, no doubt, be frustrated. I couldn't just have *something* in my hand, I had to have a concrete object – a specific *something* – like any of the ones you guessed I did. "Something" is not a thing but a sort of placeholder that has to be filled by some specific object or other. And, in this respect, it is just like "nothing."

So now we understand the error that Sal and Frankie made when they tried to *do nothing*. The reason that you can't do nothing is that, as Sal and Frankie discover, whenever you are engaged in an activity, it must be a particular kind of *doing*. You can't just *do*.

Sal and Frankie fall prey to a misunderstanding of this sort when they attempt to do *nothing*. But the ordinary language philosophers I talked about earlier would have claimed that they didn't really solve a philosophical problem when they decided that you cannot do nothing but always have to be doing something. Rather, these philosophers would have said they *dissolved* the difficulty arising from being misled by the meaning of their words.

In chapter 3, I talked about **Wittgenstein** being an unusual philosopher because he was willing to change his mind so fundamentally. In his later philosophy, he thought that all philosophical problems were caused by a failure to pay close enough attention to the actual way in which we used our words. The philosopher's role was to expose those linguistic traps, to let the fly out of the fly bottle, as he so picturesquely put it.

Sal and Frankie were trapped in their own fly bottle when they tried to do nothing. Sal's discovery – that you can't do nothing – was a philosophical discovery, one that freed him and Frankie from the type of bewitchment that Wittgenstein and other ordinary language philosophers saw embodied in the history of philosophy.

Discussing "Nothing" with Children

You might start this discussion by asking the children what are some examples of things that they really like to do. After you amass a short list, you can ask her or them if they like doing nothing. If they say that they do, you can then ask them to think about how they can do nothing. Aren't they breathing all the time? Isn't that doing something? And so on. You might also pose the question of whether they think it is possible to do nothing and why or why not.

If they say they don't like doing nothing, then you can ask them why and your discussion will take a different, equally interesting course.

5

Knuffle Bunny

How Do You Know I'm Angry If I Don't Say So?

How do you know I'm angry if I don't say so?

Trixie, the young protagonist of Mo Willem's ingeniously illustrated book *Knuffle Bunny*, is beside herself. She accompanied her father to the Laundromat. But soon after they leave, Trixie realizes that something is wrong and tries to tell her father. Because she has not yet begun to speak, she can only use baby talk to get him to understand, but her father thinks she is only saying that they are going home, and he happily expresses his agreement.

Upset that he doesn't understand, Trixie loudly repeats what she said while gesticulating wildly. Once again, her father doesn't get it, thinking that Trixie is starting to misbehave. Having no other choice, Trixie starts wailing and then collapses into a heap. But her father remains

A Sneetch Is a Sneetch and Other Philosophical Discoveries: Finding Wisdom in Children's Literature, First Edition. Thomas E. Wartenberg. Illustrations © Joy Kinigstein.
© 2013 John Wiley & Sons, Inc. Published 2013 by John Wiley & Sons, Inc.

clueless and gets angry that he has to carry his fussy daughter all the way home.

Trixie's predicament is clearly caused by her inability to communicate to her father what is upsetting her. Because Trixie has not yet learned how to talk, she cannot tell her father what is causing her distress. All she can do is make a string of apparently meaningless sounds and use her body as a means of expression. Her clueless father understands none of this and simply assumes his daughter is once again misbehaving.

When Trixie and her exasperated father arrive home, Trixie's mother greets them in the doorway of their house, asking "Where's Knuffle Bunny?" Knuffle Bunny is the stuffed rabbit toy Trixie takes with her everywhere she goes. Her mother immediately grasps that Trixie is upset that they have left Knuffle Bunny behind. So off the three of them go to try to retrieve it.

The contrast between how Trixie's father and mother respond to her desperate attempts to communicate highlight an interesting philosophical issue in the area of the philosophy of mind. Specifically, the book highlights different ways in which we communicate with one another.

Although language is clearly a crucial means of communication, there are many other things that we can do to convey a message to someone else. When one of your friends is upset about something that you did, you probably can tell by the way that they look at you or act around you, even if they haven't explicitly told you what's bothering them. You might even approach them and ask them what's wrong, despite the fact that they have not told you that something was. We don't have to speak in order to communicate with each other.

What can Trixie's predicament tell us about the significance of language and its relationship to the mind? In the seventeenth and eighteenth centuries, philosophers imagined that words were just labels that we applied to ideas that already existed in our minds. To them, language didn't seem all that important, just a means for communicating our ideas to others. Most contemporary philosophers, however, think that language has a much more basic role to play in our ability to conceptualize the world.

Clearly, because she could not speak, Trixie had difficulty communicating to her father that they had left Knuffle Bunny at the Laundromat. Think of everything she did to try to communicate that fact to him and the various ways in which he misinterpreted what she was doing. She utters sounds. She gesticulates wildly. She cries. She pouts. She refuses to budge. Yet despite all that, her father can't understand what she is trying to communicate to him. He only gets progressively more upset with her for her apparently erratic behavior.

Philosophy of Mind

The *philosophy of mind* investigates questions about the nature of the human mind. Although many different issues are addressed in this area of philosophy, the one that traditionally took pride of place was that of articulating the difference between the mind and the body, and deciding whether either was more basic than the other. This is an important philosophical issue for it addresses the question of what type of being humans are and whether it makes sense for us to see ourselves as simply one being among many others.

One important view about the nature of the human being was put forward by **René Descartes**, the father of modern Western philosophy, who claimed that the mind and the body were two fundamentally different substances that nevertheless could interact with one another. He even thought he had discovered the place in the brain – the pineal gland – where such interaction took place. Ever since, philosophers have debated whether to accept Descartes's *dualism*. Some, like the *idealist* **Bishop Berkeley**, denied that there were really physical objects, while others, like the *materialist* **Thomas Hobbes**, thought that reality consisted only of material things. Many philosophers influenced by the success of modern science accepted some form of the *materialism* advocated by Hobbes, attempting to show how the existence of the human mind could be squared with a "hard-nosed" scientific approach.

In recent years, philosophers have begun paying a great deal of attention to research in cognitive psychology. Cognitive psychologists investigate the relationship between the brain and the mind, and have shown how various mental phenomena are correlated with activity in different parts of the brain.

Virtually every field of philosophy that has been affected by new discoveries about how the brain works. But no field has been transformed as much as the philosophy of mind, which now is filled with interesting research results from cognitive psychology. Many philosophers now believe that empirical research about how the brain works has to be taken into account in our theorizing about our minds and how they function.

Why was it so hard for Trixie to communicate with her father? The philosophers from earlier centuries – who thought that human beings had a sort of internal mental language composed of different ideas – would have viewed Trixie's difficulty as stemming from her attaching the wrong sounds (words?) to the ideas she had in her mind. Here's how they would have analyzed Trixie's uttering the sound, "aggle." Because Trixie already had a complete set of mental ideas, what she was learning to do while she was learning to speak was to remember which sounds are conventionally associated with which mental idea. So when she uttered the sound "aggle," she might have made the mistake of thinking that the sound was the one that English-speakers associated with their idea of missing. Of course, she's wrong. But the question is whether this view of her mistake is persuasive.

Twentieth-century philosophers found this view unconvincing. They thought that the seventeenth- and eighteenth-century "idea" philosophers put the cart before the horse, so to speak. These more recent philosophers denied the existence of a mysterious mental realm of ideas that exists completely formed prior to the acquisition of language. They thought that language was so basic and its acquisition so revolutionary that a person acquires the ability to think specific thoughts only once they have acquired an ability to use the language with which to express them.

So, instead of seeing Trixie as being able to use her mental ideas to form the thought, "Knuffle Bunny is missing," even though she couldn't express it linguistically, twentieth-century philosophers would suggest that the sounds coming from her mouth that Willems represents as word-like – "Aggle, flaggle, klabble!" – are more similar to simple cries of distress – "Waaahhh!" – that are not linguistic in nature. These cries are forms of behavior that are tied to emotional states and serve a communicative purpose, but they are not language.

Language does have an expressive aspect, as we saw in chapter 3. For example, you might scream "Ow!" if you accidentally burned your hand while cooking dinner. Clearly, you would be expressing the fact that you are in pain. You might also shake your hand, jump up and down, and, in general, behave in pain-expressing ways. Saying, "Ow!", is just one aspect of this general pain-expressing behavior. So it's very different from saying, "My hand is really hurting because I burned it on the pot I was using to steam corn." Although your complex sentence does not convey any more about the precise emotional state you are in than your cry does, it does convey a lot of specific information about the cause of your pain-state, namely that you burned your hand on a pot.

The reason that this is relevant to Trixie's case is that it makes us wonder whether the sounds issuing from her mouth really are what we might call "proto-words," meaning sounds that are on the way to becoming words but are attached to the wrong mental ideas, as philosophers from earlier time-periods thought. Might it not be more reasonable to assimilate those sounds to screams, that is, to non-linguistic behavior tied to the expression of a specific feeling or emotion?

On the other hand, Trixie's "aggle flaggle klabble" is not a sound that we conventionally recognize as a distress cry. When she breaks down in frustration at her father's denseness and cries, Trixie is exhibiting behavior that we can recognize as expressing a negative emotional state like pain or frustration, but that's not the case for the sounds she utters. At a minimum, her use of those sounds mimics the sort of behavior she sees her parents engage in when they speak to one another, so that she is well on the road to acquiring language, a fact we know to be true from the end of the story.

When Trixie and her parents return to the Laundromat, they find Knuffle Bunny in the washing machine, where it had been left. Upon seeing her precious stuffed animal, Trixie responds, "Knuffle Bunny!" Her traumatic experience has helped her attain the linguistic skill that she had earlier needed.

Can Trixie's predicament and subsequent development help us decide whether the views of the earlier or more contemporary philosophers about the relation of language and the mind are correct? You'll recall that seventeenth- and eighteenth-century philosophers thought that children possessed a full set of mental ideas to which they only needed to attach the right sounds, i.e. words. If this is so, then "Aggle flaggle klabble!" would be an attempt to communicate a set of mental ideas that Trixie has. But can you tell which of the following statements is the one that Trixie is trying to find words to express?

1. "Knuffle Bunny is missing."
2. "We left Knuffle Bunny behind."
3. "My stuffed animal is not here."

It seems to me that all of these interpretations are more or less equally plausible ways of construing her cry. But this suggests that language is more than just a means for expressing mental ideas, for, in the absence of language, the ideas are simply not completely specific.

In fact, each of the "words" Trixie utters sounds so much like the other ones that they resemble cries of distress more than the conventional sounds that are used in linguistic utterances. "Knuffle" and "bunny," on the other hand, are quite distinct sounds that require her to use her mouth in very different ways.

So even though we can communicate with one another by a variety of means other than using words, Trixie's story shows us how important words are for communicating very specific information to someone else. Although you might be able to tell what I am feeling with a great deal of accuracy by observing my facial expressions and behavior, noticing them does not help you understand the cause of my behavior. That's part of the problem Trixie's father faces, though his obtuseness has other facets to it. He eventually sees that Trixie is upset but can't determine why from observing her frantic arm movements and cries.

Trixie's inability to communicate the cause of her distress to her father thus provides an occasion for thinking about the nature of the human mind. Feelings are an important component of our mental life and we can express those feelings in different ways. Our behavior can convey to others what we feel and one form of our behavior is linguistic. When we use language, we don't just express our feelings, but provide others with a great deal of additional information, such as the cause of our feeling a certain way. Language provides human beings with a more adequate means of communicating with one another that those provided by non-linguistic behavior on its own. In the philosophy of mind, philosophers discuss the relationship between the variety of mental contents, such as feelings and thoughts, the latter being the sorts of things that can be expressed using words.

Discussing the Philosophy of Mind with Children

You might begin your discussion of the philosophy of mind by asking whether the noises that Trixie makes are more like shaking your hand if you hit it accidentally with a hammer or more like actually saying something? If the children say the former, you can ask about the relationship they see between such expressive behavior and language itself. If they say the latter, you can ask them what she is saying, proposing alternative interpretations like the ones I suggested in the chapter. The goal of the discussion is to reflect on the nature of language in relationship to other means we have for expressing ourselves.

6

Many Moons

Do Experts Really Know More?

Do experts really know more?

The subject of James Thurber's satirical tale, *Many Moons*, is knowledge: who has it and how they acquire it. When the story begins, trouble is brewing in the kingdom, for the Princess Lenore has gotten a stomach-ache from eating "a surfeit" of strawberries. When her father, the King, asks her what would make her well, Lenore answers, "The Moon." Facing a difficult, if not impossible, request, the King asks his trusted counselors for advice.

First up is the Lord High Chamberlain. After reciting a list of everything he has previously done for the King – including obtaining ivory and pink elephants – he replies that he can't get the moon. The moon, he says, is 35,000 miles away, bigger than Lenore's room, and made of molten copper. The King is furious. He dismisses the Lord High Chamberlain and calls for the Royal Wizard.

A Sneetch Is a Sneetch and Other Philosophical Discoveries: Finding Wisdom in Children's Literature,
First Edition. Thomas E. Wartenberg. Illustrations © Joy Kinigstein.
© 2013 John Wiley & Sons, Inc. Published 2013 by John Wiley & Sons, Inc.

Despite all his magical talent and all his previous achievements – from squeezing blood out of turnips to sourcing diving rods for unearthing precious treasure – the Royal Wizard also admits that he cannot get the moon. He explains that it is 150,000 miles away, made of green cheese, and twice as big as the palace. Once again, the King rages. He now summons the Royal Mathematician.

A nearly identical scene is repeated. The Royal Mathematician explains all the things he knows – including how far up is and the distance between the horns of a dilemma – before demurring on the King's request to get the moon. He says the moon is 300,000 miles away, flat and round like a coin, made of asbestos, and half the size of the entire kingdom. Furious at yet another failure, the King turns to the Court Jester for solace.

After hearing the King explain his plight, the Court Jester comes up with a novel idea: He'll ask the Princess Lenore both how big *she* thinks the moon is and how far away. Her answer is surprising, for Lenore says the moon is no bigger than her thumbnail and about as far away as the tree outside her window. So the Jester goes to the Royal Goldsmith and has him cast a small golden charm of the moon and put it on a golden chain that the Jester can give the Princess. Although the goldsmith thinks the object he has made is not the moon – he believes that the moon is 500,000 miles away, made of bronze, and spherical – Lenore is very happy when she receives the necklace, and she gets over her upset stomach.

In its charmingly cynical way, *Many Moons* raises important questions about the nature of knowledge and those who claim to have it. The King's three counselors all have magnificent pedigrees, long lists of things they have done and accomplished. When it comes to solving the problems arising from Princess Lenore's request for the moon, however, they are stuck. Even though the lowly Court Jester, someone whose job it is to play the fool for the King's entertainment, does not himself know how to get the moon for the Princess, he does know how to get the answer. And that is, after all, a type of knowledge.

We can understand the philosophical point that *Many Moons* makes about knowledge if we ask why the Jester is able to solve a problem that none of the King's advisors can. To answer this question, we need to unearth the different assumptions about knowledge taken for granted by the advisors and the Jester.

The Theory of Knowledge

Most of us think that we know lots of things. That the moon is hundreds of thousands of miles from the earth. That it orbits the earth about once a month. That there is a book or a screen upon which you see these words.

But how do you *know* that you know these things? After all, you haven't measured the distance between the moon and the earth. You may also have seen science fiction movies in which the moon stopped orbiting the earth because of some great disaster. And the 1999 Hollywood movie *The Matrix* made everyone wonder whether the entire physical universe was a just figment of our imaginations, created by a bunch of malicious computers.

The theory of knowledge attempts to explain the nature and extent of human knowledge. The field is bedeviled by the possibility of *skepticism*, the claim that we don't really know what we think we do. Most philosophers deny at least some of the claims that skeptics make, like the ones in the preceding paragraph.

Relativism is another problem debated in the theory of knowledge. A relativist holds that knowledge claims are made relative to a basic framework, and that it is not legitimate to make cross-framework comparisons. So a traditional Christian can be justified in believing that the world was created in seven days, even though adherents of modern science claim that the universe evolved over billions of years. Many philosophers reject relativism as incoherent, claiming, among other things, that relativism cannot even be stated consistently.

There are many other issues in the theory of knowledge besides skepticism and relativism. Among them is that of developing a definition of knowledge. Although philosophers had accepted an analysis of knowledge as justified true belief since the time of **Plato**, recent work has thrown the adequacy of this account into doubt.

Because Western philosophy began in Greece more than 2,700 years ago, many philosophical terms reflect that origin. So instead of talking about the theory of knowledge, philosophers often talk about *epistemology*, a word derived from the ancient Greek word *episteme*, meaning knowledge.

The King's advisors each believe that there are clear matters of fact about the size, distance, and composition of the moon and that they are each in possession of them. They operate with what philosophers call an *objectivist* conception of knowledge, according to which there are definite facts and a knowledgeable person can know them to be true. Those who don't grasp the facts are simply in error.

An objectivist sees knowledge as something that is independent of any individual's point of view. Think about something you know, such as that the moon revolves around the earth. If you think that this is a fact, one that you know to be true, then you are an objectivist. If anyone disagrees with you about the motion of the moon around the earth, as an objectivist you would simply say they were wrong.

The Jester has a different conception of knowledge. Knowing the King's advisors to be wise men, he thinks everything each of them says must be true. But each has claimed that the moon is a different distance from the earth, a different size, and made out of a different substance. How can these conflicting statements *all* be true? They can be if the Jester is an epistemological *relativist*.

Relativists think that knowledge claims are all made from within a particular framework and that their truth can only be assessed relative to that framework. If you are working within a mathematical-scientific framework, the relativist would say, then it is true that the earth revolves around the sun. But there are other frameworks that are equally valid and in some of them, such as a traditional Western religious one, it is the sun that revolves around the earth. After all, the Bible states that the earth is the center of the universe. Because people operate within different frameworks and these frameworks support different beliefs, relativists believe that there is no truth that is absolute or framework independent. There is no way to assess the truth of a statement except relative to the framework within which it is located.

So when the King's counselors claim that the moon is made of molten copper, green cheese, and asbestos, these statements can all be true only if the truth of each can be determined only within the framework from which it is made. Take the Royal Wizard. He believes in the existence of magic. His claims to knowledge must, according to the relativist, be assessed in relation to a *magical* framework, one in which magic is seen as a real phenomenon. When the Wizard squeezed blood from a turnip, he would say that was the result of magic. A scientist like the Royal Astronomer, however, would look for physical causes for this unusual event because, according to the scientific framework, there must be physical causes for everything that happens. From a relativistic point of view, both the Wizard's and the Astronomer's claims can be true so long as they are attributed to different frameworks.

Because the Jester accepts a relativist conception of knowledge, he realizes that the Princess Lenore's request and her understanding of the nature of the moon must be understood relative to *her* framework of knowledge. The best way for him to gain access to her beliefs is to ask her what they are. The Jester's wisdom therefore is the result of his acceptance of a relativistic conception of knowledge. It's for this reason that the Jester asks the Princess what she believes about the moon, for he needs to understand her epistemic framework in order to see if her desire can be satisfied.

Once he asks the Princess about her own view, he finds out that her request for the moon is not as outlandish as it appeared. Consider first the Princess's beliefs about the size, distance, and composition of the moon: that it is smaller than her thumbnail, only as far away as the tree outside her window, and made of gold. From our perspective, all of these beliefs are clearly false, for modern science tells us that the moon is composed of various minerals, is approximately 2,160 miles wide, and averages a distance of about 240,000 miles from the earth. I assume that most of us accept the truth of what scientists tell us about such matters.

Even though the Princess's beliefs about the moon are quite unusual, she has an explanation for each one that shows the reasoning process she employed. She says that the moon is smaller than her thumbnail, for when she holds her thumb up, it covers the whole moon. Similarly, she thinks the moon is only as far away as the tree outside her window because the moon "gets caught" in the tree. And although she doesn't explain the rationale for her belief that the moon is made of gold, it seems less unmotivated than her other beliefs since poets, among others, have made this very claim, albeit metaphorically.

Although we now understand the reasoning process by means of which the Princess arrives at her beliefs, that doesn't make them true. But I would like to go beyond simply denying their truth and explain how the Princess's beliefs are the result of some interesting philosophical errors. In the first chapter, I discussed the distinction between an object and its appearance. The Princess Lenore has made the philosophical error of mistaking the appearance of the moon for the moon itself. While she can block out the appearance of the moon by holding up her thumb, it's the appearance of the moon and not the moon itself that she is blocking out. It still shines, even if she can't see it. So she is right about the size (and distance) of the *appearance* of the moon, even though what she says about the moon itself is wrong.

Lest you think that mistaking the appearance of the moon for the moon itself shows the Princess to be hopelessly naive and deluded, most of us make similar "mistakes" all the time. We all say that we see the sun rise in the east and set in the west, and that it moves across the sky during the interval between those events. But we all know – at least if we trust what science tells us – that it is the earth that is moving relative to the sun and not the other way around. We can express this point by saying that the appearance of the sun moves across the sky, while the sun itself is stationary in relation to the earth. Although we are generally more sophisticated than the Princess in that we recognize that saying the sun rose or set is just a figure of speech, this doesn't change the fact that we are speaking in a misleading manner. This raises questions about how our linguistic practices impact our beliefs, a philosophical topic we have been discussing over the course of the last few chapters.

Princess Lenore differs from the rest of us only in taking a figure of speech literally. In fact, a great deal of the humor of *Many Moons* comes from the delightful way in which Thurber is able to weave such literal-mindedness into the story unobtrusively. I hope you smiled when, for example, the Royal Mathematician boasted of measuring the distance between the horns of a dilemma. Even the King's advisor takes figures of speech literally.

In the case of the Princess, her thralldom to the literal results in some obviously mistaken beliefs about the moon. What about one of her other beliefs, the one that gave the book its title: that there are many moons and not just one? How has the Princess arrived at this erroneous belief?

Once again, Princess Lenore explains to the Jester the reasoning process that led her to this belief. She patiently tells him that every time you lose a tooth, a new one grows in its place, that when a unicorn loses its horn in the forest it grows a new one, and that when a flower is cut from a plant, a new one takes its place. The Princess reasons that the moon must also be what philosophers call "a multiple," something that has a variety of different instances.

The Princess has here employed *analogical reasoning* to justify her belief. She uses facts about three other objects – teeth, unicorn horns, and flowers – as the basis for her belief about the moon. We will explore problems with analogical reasoning in the next chapter. Here, it's enough to point out that "the Moon" refers to a single object and not, as "teeth," "horn," and "flower" do, to an entire class. This difference undercuts the attempt to reason analogically.

One reason Lenore may have been led astray is the similarity between the term "the Moon" and others like "the lion." The term "the lion" refers not to an individual lion such as Simba (from *The Lion King*) but to lions in general. So if I say, "The lion is the king of beasts," I am making a claim about lions as a class, as opposed to tigers, giraffes, elephants, and other animals, not about the individual Simba.

But the term "the moon" is different. Although astronomers use the word "moon" to refer to natural satellites of celestial objects, when we say "*the* moon," we are not referring to that class of objects. Rather, we are referring to one specific moon, the one that revolves around our own home, the earth.

A question about the consistency of my approach to this story needs to be addressed before we can leave *Many Moons*. I said that the Jester was a wise man because of his relativistic view of knowledge. But I then criticized the Princess's beliefs in a way that presumed the truth of objectivism. Aren't I being inconsistent?

I don't think so. While I admit that relativism provides us with some insights, I don't accept it as a general theory of knowledge and neither do most philosophers. What relativism does very well is warn us about the danger of assuming you have exclusive possession of the truth in regard to some issue or type of knowledge – the *epistemic vice* that the King's advisors suffer from. The Jester is more humble, realizing that everyone has his or own reasons for their beliefs. His willingness to go to the Princess to ask her to explain her beliefs is a healthy alternative to the dogmatic assertions of the counselors.

But we can, of course, accept the importance of epistemic humility without embracing epistemic relativism whole hog. In fact, if you accepted my analysis of the errors that led to the Princess's *false* beliefs about the moon, you must have at least implicitly rejected relativism. My analysis only makes sense if you assume that there is *a truth* about such matters.

Discussing the Theory of Knowledge with Children

A good place to begin this discussion is with the Princess Lenore's beliefs about the moon. You might ask whether the children agree with Lenore about the size, distance, and composition of the moon, as well as to the possibility of there being more than one of them. You might also ask them if they think that the Jester is smarter than the King and all of his advisors and, if they do, why this is so.

7

Yellow and Pink

Could Human Life Have Arisen Purely by Chance?

Could human life have arisen purely by chance?

As we saw in the last chapter, philosophers are very interested in the reasons we have for our beliefs. One of the beliefs most hotly debated by philosophers is that about the existence or non-existence of God. In William Steig's inventive book, *Yellow and Pink*, the debate is played out through a dialogue between two painted wooden puppets.

The story begins with the two puppets lying on a piece of newspaper. As they look around, they wonder how they got there and what their purpose is. These are traditional philosophical questions, ones that almost all of us find ourselves pondering at some time during our lives. In fact, philosophy is born out of our attempt to answer such fundamental questions.

One source for a belief in God is that His very existence is thought to provide an answer to these pressing questions. If there is a God and we can decipher His intentions, many people think we would then be able to understand what the point of our lives is.

A Sneetch Is a Sneetch and Other Philosophical Discoveries: Finding Wisdom in Children's Literature, First Edition. Thomas E. Wartenberg. Illustrations © Joy Kinigstein.
© 2013 John Wiley & Sons, Inc. Published 2013 by John Wiley & Sons, Inc.

Philosophy of Religion

The question of whether God exists is one of the basic questions about human existence. Traditionally, philosophers developed proofs to demonstrate that He did. Whether such proofs actually prove what they set out to is one of the fundamental questions in the *philosophy of religion*, the field of philosophy that addresses questions about faith and its relation to reason, among other things.

The history of Western philosophy includes a variety of different challenges to religious belief. One of the strongest comes from natural science. If the world can be completely explained in naturalistic terms, that is, via physics, biology, and other sciences, what room is there left for God?

Although believers (known as *theists*) attempt to show that God can still play a role in human experience by helping us understand the world despite the reach of natural science, those who deny God's existence (*atheists*) argue that belief in God is irrational. One of the most famous atheists was philosopher **David Hume**, who claimed that no rational grounds could be given for religious belief.

A further question, apart from whether God actually exists, is whether human beings can have knowledge of his existence. Generally, contemporary philosophers assume that such knowledge cannot come from direct acquaintance with Him, although there are people who believe that God has contacted them directly and traditional religious documents like *The Bible* testify to such interactions. But since most philosophers are skeptical of this idea – at least for themselves and their contemporaries – the fundamental concern of contemporary philosophers is whether God's existence can be *proven* or not. Even though we can't learn about God's existence through our senses, reason might be able to show us that God exists, according to theists.

The Danish philosopher **Søren Kierkegaard** famously denied that religious faith was based upon reason, so that trying to prove God's existence was beside the point. Kierkegaard's concept of the *leap of faith* sought to explain how faith was possible in a world dominated by reason – and, hence, science.

In the book, Yellow (the yellow-colored puppet) is skeptical of the existence of a God-like creator. Pink, on the other hand believes in the existence of one. He tells Yellow that someone had to have made them because their complex structure could only be the result of intentional decisions of their creator.

Yellow is struck by Pink's observations, but remains skeptical. He first asks why, if someone created them, they would just be left there without any explanation for why they existed; he decides that the two of them must have come into existence as a result of pure chance.

Pink can't believe it. Laughing, he points out to Yellow that he has various different parts that seem to be fitted together into a well-designed whole. He finds preposterous the idea that this could just have happened accidentally.

Yellow tells Pink to stop his laughing. Over the course of millions of years, he says, many unusual things could have occurred. Out of the millions and billions of things that took place during that time period, why couldn't there have been one occurrence that resulted in their coming to be? Because the world has existed for so many years, coincidences such as the one that created them are very likely to have happened.

Pink remains skeptical, forcing Yellow to elaborate his view. Couldn't a branch have broken off of a tree, Yellow asks. And, when it fell, split open into the right shape for a pair of legs? And then, during the winter, if the wood froze and split, a mouth could have been formed. Yellow continues speculating about how he could have come into existence and invents a story in which all sorts of natural *accidents* result in his existence, from blowing sand smoothing out his surface to lightning making arms, fingers, and toes.

Pink points out that there are many details that Yellow's story leaves unexplained. When he asks Yellow to account for eyes, ears, and nostrils – features that don't seem purely coincidental to him – Yellow responds that insects and woodpeckers might have been responsible, or even perhaps hailstones. It seems Yellow can find a solution to any of the problems that Pink throws up. Pink responds by asking him how, even if this could have happened *once*, his account can explain the existence of the two of them? To which Yellow simply reiterates that, given the immense amount of time he's talking about, the accidents that brought one of them into existence could have occurred more than once.

Unbowed, Pink takes another tack. What about the differences between them? What accounts for that? Exactly, Yellow surprisingly responds, suggesting that they probably came from different types of wood. Their dissimilarities actually confirm his theory rather than refuting it, for it shows that their differences have an origin, something that remains inexplicable within Pink's creator theory. When Pink continues to press Yellow about their colors and the buttons placed so symmetrically on their torsos, Yellow is puzzled. Some things will have to remain a mystery, he admits. But that doesn't defeat his appeal to chance as the factor responsible for their existence.

Pink represents, of course, the traditional theist, someone who believes in the existence of God. Traditional theists also hold that their faith is rational, since God's existence can be proven. Not all theists agree, for some, like **Kierkegaard**, hold that belief in God is a matter of faith. But through the centuries, many philosophers have advanced proofs of God's existence in light of their view that there is a rational foundation for the belief in the existence of God.

There are a variety of different strategies that philosophers and theologians in the Western tradition have used to try and prove the existence of God. All of these proofs assume, more or less, a Western, that is Judeo-Christian-Islamic, conception of God. My discussion will focus on proofs within this broad tradition.

Here are three different types of proofs for the existence of God:

- The *ontological proof*, first presented by **St Anselm of Canterbury**, starts out with the concept of God as the greatest of all beings and argues that a being so defined must necessarily exist. The word "ontological" comes from the Greek for being (*onta*).
- The *cosmological proof* begins with the idea that our own existence is *contingent*, that we might never have existed. It then argues that a world cannot be composed exclusively of contingent beings, that there must be a being whose existence is *necessary*. To adherents of this argument, God is simply that necessary being, the being who could not *not* have existed. As with the ontological proof, the name is derived from a Greek word, this time meaning the world (*kosmos*).
- The proof that many consider the most convincing is the one that proceeds from the incredible orderliness found in the natural world. This is the *argument from design*, and it's a version of this argument that Pink puts forward. He is impressed by the way in which everything in the world seems to be fit together purposively, arguing that such coordination must be the result of conscious design.

Many people wonder at the amazing things they see in nature. Perhaps looking at a sunset or a beautiful lake or a snow-covered mountain, you have been struck by the beauty and symmetry of all the elements of the scene. The argument from design asserts that the beauty and perfection that you picked up on must have come about through the actual efforts of some type of designer. And, of course, this designer is taken to be none other than God himself, all-powerful, all-knowing, and beneficent.

The argument from design was put forward by philosophers as early as **Plato** and continued to exert an influence through the centuries. Its influence reached its peak in the thought of **Gottfried Wilhelm Leibniz**, who asserted not just that this world was the result of God's decision to create it, but that it was the best of all possible worlds, a view know as *optimism*. This characterization is the result of Leibniz's belief that, despite all the pain and suffering there is in the world, this is the best of all possible worlds and God chose to create it for that reason.

This argument from design has not been without its critics. **David Hume** was one of its most vocal opponents. He thought that there were some fundamental logical flaws in the proof that rendered it invalid.

The first problem Hume identified was that, even if one granted the validity of the argument, it did not prove what it set out to. The most the argument could prove was the existence of an *Architect* of the world, not God as traditionally conceived by Western religions. That is, the being whose existence the proof purports to prove lacks many of the characteristics customarily thought to be essential to God. For example, the proof could not demonstrate that God was all-powerful, only that he was powerful enough to create the world. Hume maintained that, even if you granted the theist the validity of the argument from design, it would not result in establishing the existence of God as traditionally conceived, but at most a being with characteristics quite distinct from His.

Hume claimed that there is an even more serious problem with the logical structure of the proof. As Hume correctly notes, the argument from design is based on pointing out similarities between entities in the natural world (supposedly created by God) and objects that have been created by a human being. In Leibniz's version, for instance, he explicitly likens the world to a painting, clearly the product of purposeful human activity. This is an example of an *analogical* argument. It compares one thing with another and bases its conclusion upon their similarity – in this case that the natural world must have a creator, just as a painting does.

This is what Hume objects to. He points out that there are many examples of bad analogical arguments. We have already encountered one in the previous chapter. In order to justify her belief that there were many moons, the Princess Lenore compared the moon to a tooth, a unicorn's horn, and a flower. With those objects, Lenore says, when one disappears, another one takes its place. So it must be with the moon, she mistakenly concludes; when one sets, a new and different one is ready to rise the next evening.

The problem with this argument – aside from its dependence on a mythical being – is that the moon is not like a tooth or a flower. Basing one's argument on a similarity between certain things overlooks ways in which they differ. Analogical arguments are very dangerous and usually lead to unjustified conclusions.

Consider the following analogical argument:

Potassium cyanide is like sugar.
It's fine to add sugar to my coffee.
Therefore, it's fine to add potassium cyanide to my coffee.

Clearly, there are important differences between potassium cyanide and sugar that defeat this argument – just as there are differences between the moon and a tooth. One is the fact that potassium cyanide is poisonous, whereas sugar is not. So even though the two look quite similar, we can't treat them interchangeably.

Hume rejects the argument from design because of the faulty analogy it employs. He points out that there are differences – or *disanalogies* – between the world and human creations such as paintings that defeat the validity of the argument. For one thing, we can recognize artifacts – the products of human design – because they differ from other things like stones that are not created by human beings. But in the case of the world, there is only one, so there is nothing with which to contrast it. We cannot judge the world to have been the product of design if there are not other, similar objects that we judge not to have been.

Hume's thinking parallels that of Yellow in many respects. At the core of Yellow's argument is the idea that we don't need to assume the existence of God in order to account for the order and structure of the universe. The commonly accepted philosophical principle *Ockham's razor*, named after the medieval philosopher **William of Ockham**, says that we should not assume the existence of objects beyond those that are necessary in our theories. God, according to Hume, is one such superfluous object.

In order for objections to the argument from design to be fully convincing they must offer some alternate account of the origin of things in the world.

Yellow does just that with his account of how he and Pink could have come into being through a series of coincidences. Yellow's story is reminiscent of Darwin's theory of evolution. Like Yellow, Darwin does not attempt to account for the existence of the physical universe. His concern is with biological creatures and, ultimately, human beings. If we accept a theory like Darwin's, we can explain how human beings and other species came into existence in a purely *naturalistic* manner, that is, without having to make recourse to any being outside of the natural order who guides its development.

The key notion in Darwin's theory, as in Yellow's, is *accident*. But the particular type of accident Darwin's theory requires is a *mutation*. A mutation is an accidental change in the nature of an organism. According to Darwin's theory, some mutations are beneficial to the organism that results from the mutation because it gives the new organism a survival advantage over the old.

Such mutations are then *selected for* in evolution, with the result that a new species comes into being over many generations. This is, in its very basic outline, a theory like Yellow's, one that makes no reference to a divine being who brings human beings (or wooden puppets!) into existence.

Many contemporary philosophers think that Darwin's theory of evolution, along with Hume's critique of the validity of the proof, cuts the ground out from under the argument from design. However, this does not mean that one is forced on logical grounds to deny the existence of God. Remember, many people simply deny that belief in God can be justified by rational argument. For them, belief in God is a matter of faith. The weaknesses in the argument from design do nothing to affect beliefs grounded in this way. Nor do they show that God's existence cannot be proven in another manner.

William Steig may well have had this in mind when he wrote the surprise ending to *Yellow and Pink*. Suddenly, a long-haired human being appears on the scene and picks up the two wooden puppets. He notes that their paint has dried, so he turns around and heads back into his house, his two creations in hand. Both Yellow and Pink are puzzled by who he could be.

Discussing Arguments for the Existence of God with Children

In discussing arguments for God's existence with children, it's important to acknowledge that the issue at hand is not whether God exists, but whether a specific attempt to prove His existence is convincing. You can criticize the argument from design, for example, without being an atheist.

After emphasizing this, why not ask the children whether they find Yellow or Pink's argument more convincing? In developing their answers, make sure that they understand the details of each argument. Is there anything that either argument cannot fully explain? Do they have to make an *ad hoc* assumption, that is, an assumption that has no other purpose than to explain what it is supposed to explain?

8

Morris the Moose

How Do You Know When You've Made a Mistake?

How do you know when you've made a mistake?

In assessing Princess Lenore's beliefs about the moon in chapter 6, we saw that people could have mistaken beliefs that they arrive at by faulty reasoning. B. Wiseman's delightful book, *Morris the Moose*, takes a more detailed look at such reasoning, itself the subject of *philosophical logic*.

On the first page we meet Morris, a cartoonishly drawn moose, looking at a cow. Morris greets the cow by telling her she is a funny-looking moose, to which the cow replies, "I am a cow not a moose."

Morris isn't swayed. He explains to the cow why she *must* be a moose: she has four legs, a tail, and "things on her head" (i.e. horns). When Morris continues to defend his obviously false idea, he does something very important in philosophical terms: He backs up his belief that the cow is a moose with *reasons*.

A Sneetch Is a Sneetch and Other Philosophical Discoveries: Finding Wisdom in Children's Literature, First Edition. Thomas E. Wartenberg. Illustrations © Joy Kinigstein.
© 2013 John Wiley & Sons, Inc. Published 2013 by John Wiley & Sons, Inc.

Logic

Morris the moose draws a false conclusion from true premises: that the cow has four legs, a tail, and horns. His problem could have been remedied by paying more attention to *logic*.

Logic is the most fundamental area of philosophy, because all reasoning must accord with its norms or standards. **Aristotle** first developed a system of logical reasoning. Philosophers didn't notice that his system was based on a mistaken assumption until the late nineteenth century when an obscure Austrian mathematician and philosopher, **Gottlob Frege**, made that discovery. All subsequent developments in logic are based upon Frege's systematization of the discipline.

Although logic often resembles mathematics in its abstract characterization of reasoning, *informal logic* focuses on how we reason in ordinary life. It turns out that people often reason fallaciously, for the standards for correct reasoning are not always obvious.

Take the difference between a necessary and a sufficient condition. **A** is a *necessary* condition for **B** just in case something cannot be **B** without also being **A**. Consider being female and being pregnant. Being female is a necessary condition for being pregnant because if something is pregnant, then it must be female. On the other hand, **C** is a *sufficient* condition for **D** just in case something being **C** entails it's also **D**. Driving in a car is a sufficient condition for getting to the post office, because driving is one of the ways you can get to the post office. But if you are at the post office, it doesn't mean that you drove there, for you might have walked or biked.

There are many other common logical fallacies. One is *begging the question* or assuming what you want to prove. If you assume something, that doesn't provide an independent reason for believing it. Another, the fallacy of *composition*, stems from assuming the whole has the same properties as the parts. An omelet made from good ingredients is not necessarily a good omelet.

Learning how to spot fallacies is an important skill to acquire. If you try to spot fallacies in newspapers or magazines, you may be surprised at their frequency.

What exactly is a reason for a belief and why are they so important to philosophers? All of us believe lots of different things all of the time. Right now, as you read this book, you see words upon a page or screen. So you have the *belief* that there are words in front of your eyes that you are reading. This is an example of a *perceptual belief*, a belief that is generated and supported by what you see. You *believe* that there are words there for you to read because you *see* them.

We each have many beliefs that we take to be justified because they are supported by our current perceptions. But not all beliefs are justified in this way. Take Morris's belief that the cow is a moose. He doesn't just say that it's true because he sees a moose there in front of him. He provides reasons for his belief: She has four legs, a tail, and horns. And he's right about all of those things. The question is, "Do these three criteria justify Morris saying that the cow is a moose?"

Although Wiseman doesn't explain why Morris takes those three criteria to justify his belief, he evidently believes that anything that has four legs, a tail, and horns is a moose. (Later in the story, when Morris encounters a deer, he reasons in the same way, supporting the attribution of this belief to him.) He takes these three criteria to be adequate for determining which animals are moose: ones with four legs, a tail, and horns. Of course, since we know that the cow is *not* a moose, there must be something wrong with Morris's approach. Let's see if the cow herself can throw some light on that.

After Morris tells the cow why she has to be a moose, she presents three facts about herself that explain why she is a cow (and not a moose): She moos, she gives milk to humans, and her mother is a cow. In effect, she is saying, "Look, Morris, I may have the three properties you say I do, but that does not mean I am a moose. In fact, here are three other features that I have that cows have but moose do not. And that's why I'm a cow and not a moose."

The cow is clearly contesting the adequacy of Morris's criteria for determining which animals are moose, for moose do not moo, they do not give milk to humans, and they do not have cows for mothers. So the cow is not just saying that Morris is wrong about the type of animal she is, she is also saying that Morris is wrong about his claim about what criteria establish that an animal is a moose. In short, Morris has made a *logical* blunder.

Logicians would characterize Morris's mistake as taking a *necessary* condition for being a moose to be a *sufficient* condition. If something is a necessary condition for being a moose, then nothing can be a moose without having it. Think about having four legs – and let's not worry about exceptions, such as moose that have lost their legs in hunters' traps. Nothing can be a moose without having four legs, so having four legs is a necessary condition for being a moose. But lots of creatures have four legs and are *not* moose, so having four legs is not a sufficient condition for being a moose. A creature needs to have a lot more characteristics besides having four legs in order to be a moose. And also having a tail and antlers are not *jointly sufficient* for making a creature a moose, either. For a number of features to be jointly sufficient for making a creature a moose, anything that had those features could not fail to be moose. In fact, though, only a biologist might be able list all the features that are *jointly sufficient* to make a creature a moose.

Morris is not alone in his tendency to conflate these two different types of conditions. People do it all the time. It's true that oxygen is necessary for human life. But that doesn't mean that, if someone dies, they did so because of a lack of oxygen. There are many other things that can cause a person to die. Nor does it mean that oxygen is sufficient for human life. An oxygen-rich atmosphere would not support life if the atmospheric temperature were extremely hot or cold.

As it turns out, Morris himself is not cowed (sorry!) by the cow's response to him. He has answers to everything she says. His responses help us come to grips with some important aspects of the theory of knowledge, which we first met in the previous chapter.

Morris's first response: When the cow says that she can moo, Morris says he can too. Morris's saying, "I can moo, too," actually demonstrates the truth of what he claims, because saying "moo" in the right way is a form of mooing. Using words in this way, to both describe and do something, is known as *performative language*. A common example is a bride or groom saying "I do."

Now you might respond that just saying "Moo" is not mooing. And of course, depending on how one said "Moo," you might be right. But our hero, Morris, might be capable of saying "Moo" in a sufficiently cow-like manner for it to qualify as being a moo and not just be a way of describing one.

Morris's second response: When the cow says that she gives milk to humans Morris is nonplussed. He simply says, "OK, then. You must be a milk-to-humans-giving moose." Instead of admitting that he was wrong, Morris just differentiates between moose that give milk to humans and moose that don't.

The Performative Use of Language

In discussing the philosophy of language in chapter 3, I avoided discussing an important feature of language, it's ability *to do* something. We considered the descriptive, evaluative, and expressive uses of language. But language also has a *performative* aspect: it can be used to do things.

One example of a performative use of language occurs when you say, "I promise." Say that a friend has told you a secret but asked you not to tell anyone. When you say, "I promise," your saying the words actually creates the promise. You are doing something with words, to invoke the title of **J.L. Austin**'s famous book about performatives.

Performatives are also associated with language used by many officials in government. A judge, for example, who says, "I sentence John Doe to five years in jail," has actually created John Doe's sentence by uttering those words. Similarly, a policeman who says, "You are under arrest," actually puts you under arrest by saying those words. This is very different from a friend who says, "You owe me $10." If you do owe your friend $10, his telling you so did not make it true. His utterance is not performative.

In recent Continental philosophy, i.e. philosophy as widely practiced in Europe, the concept of performatives has been expanded beyond its original meaning. In this usage, many different features of human beings are taken to be the result of *performativity*. So rather than taking gender, for example, to be something fixed by biology, philosophers in this tradition have argued that gender is performed, meaning that one's gender is determined by the way in which one acts.

Morris here makes an *ad hoc distinction* between milk-to-humans-giving and non-milk-to-humans-giving moose. The distinction is *ad hoc* because it has no justification other than allowing Morris to maintain his claim that the cow is a moose. As such, the distinction is not justified, for it has no independent support. For a distinction to be a valid one, it has to have some basis other than saving a theory from objections.

Morris's third response: When the cow tells Morris that she can't be a moose because her mother is a cow, Morris responds in a way that exposes another traditional philosophical issue: he presents an *argument* to show she is wrong. In effect, he says the following:

> You are a moose.
> All mothers of moose are moose.
> So your mother must be a moose.

Once again, there is a name for the logical blunder that Morris makes here. It is called *begging the question*. What's at issue in Morris's dispute with the cow is precisely whether or not she is a moose. He can't just *assume* that she's a moose and *then* show her on *that* basis that she's wrong about her mother. The cow would probably even agree that *if* she were a moose, her mother would be a moose, but she's not and so her mother's not either. Morris cannot just obstinately assert that she is one if he's trying to persuade *her* that she's wrong to claim that she is not.

Throughout, Morris holds onto his belief that the cow is a moose and finds ways to reject the cow's claim that she is not without seriously considering what she says. He is not bothered by any of the cow's assertions because he won't let them affect his belief. He just figures out ways to accommodate or reject the cow's claims without modifying his own view that she is a moose. This approach is what the important American philosopher **C.S. Peirce** called "the method of tenacity," one of several ways of justifying what you believe. According to the school of philosophy founded by Peirce – *pragmatism* – you cannot show that defending one's beliefs in this way is mistaken. So long as someone is determined to use the method of tenacity, and follows through with it, you can't prove to him that he is wrong. So long as Morris rejects the truth of enough obvious facts, like the cow's mother being a cow, the erroneous nature of his belief cannot be demonstrated to him.

So what ultimately gets Morris to change his mind and admit that he was wrong about the cow? After encountering two other animals – a deer and a horse, both of which Morris claims are moose – Morris goes to drink some water. While sipping away, he sees four reflections in the pool of water – his own and those of the cow, the deer, and the horse. He decides that none of the other animals looks like him, so they can't be moose. And that's when he realizes he made a mistake.

Let's try to reconstruct the grounds for Morris's reconsidering whether these other animals are moose or not. Morris appeals to something like the following principle:

Things that look different from each other are really different from each other.

We often appeal to principles like this in our daily lives. Say someone offers you a bowl of various fruit and you want to have an apple. You see a pear, a banana, and a cumquat. If you want an apple, you will be disappointed. It is unlikely that you would think that maybe the pear was really an apple that just happens to look like a pear. We trust appearances to signify real differences between things in the world, a point in keeping with our trust in our perceptual experience that we discussed at the start of this chapter.

Appealing as this principle is, in many circumstances it turns out to be false. Take two glasses of water, one of plain water and one in which someone has dissolved arsenic. The contents of the two glasses *appear* to be the same but they are not. We just can't see that there are arsenic molecules dissolved in the water of the second glass. Things that look the same can really be very different – and have very different effects, as drinking a glass of water laced with arsenic would attest.

On the other hand, things that appear to be different can actually be the same. Think about ice and steam. They really look like very different types of things, but we all know that they are simply two different forms of water. Our knowledge of the basic principles of changes of state allows us to see that the apparent differences between ice and steam conceal their identical chemical structure.

This line of thought must push us to say that Morris made an even bigger "MOOSEtake" by taking appearances to be an accurate guide to reality. When it comes to developing an accurate picture of reality, you can't simply trust appearances. The underlying structure of things requires reference to at least some simple theoretical explanations of why things appear the way they do.

The real lesson we can take from this story of this stubborn moose is that it can sometimes be hard to admit your mistakes. Our own beliefs have a tenacity that makes it hard to accept contradictory evidence, and we are not always open to finding the truth if it challenges our cherished beliefs.

Discussing Mistakes with Children

We saw Morris refuse to admit his mistake but, instead, take a tenacious approach that dismissed the evidence the cow supplied to show him he was wrong. You might ask whether the children have ever acted similarly. Were there any times when they held on to a cherished belief in spite of good evidence that could have showed them they were wrong? Did they eventually change their mind? What made them do so?

9

Emily's Art

What's the Difference between Saying the *Mona Lisa Is a* Great Painting and Vanilla Is Your Favorite Flavor?

What's the difference between saying the *Mona Lisa* is a great painting and vanilla is your favorite flavor?

On January 21, 2011, the *New York Times* music critic Anthony Tommasini published a list of the 10 greatest classical music composers of all time, with Bach, Beethoven, and Mozart leading the pack. As you might expect, the list generated a lot of controversy. Some people challenged the omission of specific composers like Chopin and John Cage. Others objected to way the list had been compiled, asserting that fame, supposedly one of Tommasini's criteria, was not the same thing as greatness. Still others objected to the idea that greatness could be used to judge musical works and their composers. In general, a wide-ranging brouhaha ensued. (You can find it at www.nytimes.com/2011/01/23/arts/music/23composers.html, last accessed November 20, 2012.)

When the first graders in Peter Catalanotto's delightfully illustrated picture book, *Emily's Art*, discover they will be having an art contest at the

A Sneetch Is a Sneetch and Other Philosophical Discoveries: Finding Wisdom in Children's Literature, First Edition. Thomas E. Wartenberg. Illustrations © Joy Kinigstein.
© 2013 John Wiley & Sons, Inc. Published 2013 by John Wiley & Sons, Inc.

end of the week, their reactions mirror those of Tommasini's readers: The idea of an art contest puzzles them. How can one painting be chosen as *the best*? And they remain perplexed even after their teacher, Ms Fair, explains that there will be a judge who will choose the best picture and it will get a prize ribbon in addition to being hung in the gym.

Emily, the book's young protagonist, is a good artist, and she paints a number of different pictures in preparation for the contest. Monday, it's a picture of her family at breakfast. Oddly, her mother appears in it four times. Emily explains to her best friend Kelly that's because her mother is so busy. Since it's not possible to *literally* show her mother's busyness in a painting – after all, a person's busyness can't be seen in the way that, say, red can – she has adopted an indirect strategy that allows her to represent features of her world view that cannot be directly perceived.

The next day, Emily's painting of Ms Fair shows her sporting angel wings. Again, Emily is trying to convey a feature of Ms Fair that cannot be represented in direct perceptual form, her "niceness." To communicate this non-visual feature of Ms Fair to viewers, Emily includes a symbolic visual element in the painting, i.e. the angel wings.

When Emily creates a painting of herself and Kelly on Wednesday, they are wearing the same outfits and look very much alike, despite their different hair colors. This time, Emily wants to show that they are best friends. The similarity of their appearance in the painting symbolizes the closeness of their friendship.

Finally, on Thursday Emily paints a picture of her dog, Thor, with huge ears. This time, Emily alters a physical feature of her subject in order to represent its significance. The large size of Thor's ears symbolizes his excellent hearing. This is the picture Emily chooses to submit to the contest.

Meanwhile, Emily has taught Kelly how to draw a butterfly, and Kelly draws a different colored one each day. Kelly clearly is not as skilled an artist as Emily. Rather than coming up with her own design, she slavishly follows the pattern Emily created, her own versions varying from Emily's original only in their coloring.

Even before we get to the contest – the central focus of *Emily's Art* – an interesting issue about art has arisen. Emily's drawings are unusual because Emily is not attempting to create visually accurate representations of the subjects of her paintings. Instead of adopting a straightforward *realist* approach to art, Emily includes elements in her paintings that are not directly perceivable features of her subjects. One way to characterize Emily's style would be to call it *expressionist*. This label indicates that her paintings move beyond simply depicting objects as literally and accurately as possible, and include symbolic elements that *express* her ideas and feelings about those things.

The Philosophy of Art and Aesthetics

We've all had the experience of being puzzled by works of contemporary art. Museums are filled with objects that look to many viewers as if they've been stolen from a trash heap. Are such things really works of art or are people just being fooled? And if they are art, why is that?

Questions like these are the province of the *philosophy of art*. Traditionally, the philosophy of art was also called *aesthetics*, a term derived from the ancient Greek. Aesthetics initially focused on the nature of immediate sensory experience, but narrowed to a concern with beauty and other similar properties. In the twentieth century, philosophers distinguished questions about art from broader questions about, say, the beauty inherent in a sunset or a mountain landscape.

Philosophers use the term "art" to encompass all of the different *arts*, from painting and sculpture to music, dance, theater, and film. This can be confusing, since we ordinarily associate "art" only with painting and other visual arts.

There are many intriguing issues in the philosophy of art. For example, philosophers have proposed various different solutions to the question of what art is. In addition to the traditional answer of accurate representation mentioned above, philosophers pointed to other features of art works that made them *art*: their expression of ideas or emotions; their possession of "significant form"; their embodiment of meaning. Each of these answers has been rejected for failing to adequately distinguish art objects from other things, so the question of what makes something a work of art remains hotly debated.

Another question that has provoked controversy pertains to artworks that involve fictional characters, such as novels and films. Since these characters are not real, the challenge is to explain why their fates move us? After all, if I admit that I made up a story I told you about my dying sister, you would no longer feel empathy for me but likely only anger. Why is the same not true of fictional works whose characters are no more real than my dying sister?

Emily's style of painting demonstrates the shortcomings of a view that was dominant in the philosophy of art since the time of **Plato** in the fourth century BCE. According to this view, the goal of art was to reproduce the visual appearances of objects. Until the mid nineteenth century, philosophers of art held that a painting was good in so far as it was a faithful reproduction of the person or object its depicts.

The standard of accurate representation provides a criterion for judging which of Emily's and her classmates' paintings is the best. The painting that presents the objects it depicts most accurately and realistically would win. Although people could disagree about their assessment of the realism of different paintings – you might think that Annamaire's painting of a goat was the most realistic, while I might take Kenshaw's of a boat to be – there would be a single, clear standard to use in judging the artistic merit of all paintings, including those of the children.

Emily's paintings show that this theory of art is not adequate. It would be a mistake to judge her paintings wanting because they are not realistic, for Emily does not intend each element of her paintings to be a visually accurate representation of her subject.

One might try to salvage the idea of a single standard for assessing the artistic merit of paintings by substituting *expressiveness* for accuracy of depiction. For a certain period in the history of Western art, this seemed like a reasonable proposal. Van Gogh's vibrant landscapes and Edvard Munch's canvases of tortured souls suggest that expression was the central value that paintings of the time sought to embody. Even looking back at earlier Western artists it seemed plausible to think that Raphael, Rembrandt, and others were more concerned with expressing their feelings and ideas than with simply producing accurate copies of items in the real world.

The history of Western art in the twentieth century nailed the coffin shut on this suggestion. Picasso and Braque's cubist canvases were neither realistic portrayals of objects nor expressions on any discernible ideas about them. And what about displaying a urinal (Marcel Duchamp) or a carton of Brillo soap pads (Andy Warhol)? Such attempts seemed to demonstrate that anything could be art, irrespective of what it looked like. These works didn't appear to involve expression at all.

All of this makes the question of how to judge an art contest truly fraught. There seems to be no single criterion that can be used to evaluate the artistic goodness or badness of works. No wonder Emily and her classmates were puzzled.

On the night before the art contest, Emily remains perplexed about the whole idea of judging art. What worries her is whether – and why – it makes sense to say that one painting is *the best* among a whole group of her classmates' paintings.

As she attempts to solve this puzzle, she asks her mother whether it makes sense to judge chocolate to be better than vanilla, because the cases of artistic evaluation and gustatory preference seem similar to her. But whether we prefer chocolate or vanilla is simply a matter of taste. Although one person prefers one and another prefers the other, we don't expect there to be any resolution to this disagreement. There is *no best* flavor. There are simply different flavors and different people have different preferences for one or the other. Many other comparable things are just like that: dancing or singing; the sun or the moon; soccer or basketball; hugs or tickles. Emily finds the idea of comparing all these things difficult if not incoherent because, as with tastes, there is no single standard by which they can be ranked.

Some things can be compared, so that comparative judgments make sense in regard to them. If someone asks me who is taller, me or my brother, there is a clear answer: He is. That's because there is a definite standard – our actual height – that is used as a basis for the comparison. The question raised by *Emily's Art* is whether paintings are more like tastes or heights.

The school principal's mother has been selected to judge the art contest, deemed qualified since her cousin is married to an artist. At first, she picks Emily's painting of Thor because she thinks it's such a good, realistic painting of a rabbit. What she admires are its detail and gorgeous colors. When she is told that the subject of the painting is really a dog, she is horrified. Turns out she was once bitten by one. So she pins the blue ribbon on Kelly's painting of a butterfly, murmuring that she loves butterflies.

Emily is crestfallen. And we are sympathetic because it's quite apparent that the judge made a mistake. She has used an inappropriate criterion in judging the first-graders' paintings. But why exactly is that?

Even if we are not sure exactly what the correct basis is for determining the artistic value of an artwork, the judge's error establishes that there are certain things that one should *not* use as the basis for evaluating the artistic value of works of art. The one that clearly stands out is the one the judge used: how she feels about the subject of the painting. Judging a painting of a butterfly to be better than a painting of a dog because one likes butterflies and abhors dogs is simply not the right way to determine the artistic value of the respective works. The artistic value of a work of art – which we need to distinguish from other forms of value such as, for example, a painting's economic value or price – is based on features of the work itself, and not on one's feelings about the subject of the work.

When the avant-garde artist Marcel Duchamp submitted an ordinary urinal titled "Fountain" to an exhibition, among the things he may have been trying to show was that art works are artistically valuable not for what they depict but for the nature of their depiction. If even a urinal could be a work of art, then anything can be, as the philosopher and art critic **Arthur Danto** has argued.

Although this does not settle the question of how it is possible to make distinctions about the relative artistic merit of works of art, we mustn't forget that people do this all the time – as we saw with the *New York Times* list of the top 10 greatest composers. Many lists like this seem absurd and immediately prompt questions such as, "How was the list made? What was the rationale for the choices? Does it reflect the personal preference of the list maker or something else? Most importantly, what are the criteria that were used to determine membership on the list?" The judge of the first-grade art contest talked about "detail" and "gorgeous color" as justifying her initial choice of Emily's painting for first prize. Could these be features whose presence in a painting justify a positive assessment of it?

Perhaps unfortunately, the answer is no. There are no purely descriptive features of a work of art that contribute unambiguously to its artistic value. You'll recall the distinction between descriptive and evaluative properties from my discussion of *Shrek!* in the third chapter. In the present context, the descriptive features of a work of art are those features that are directly perceivable, such as its color, shape, texture. The evaluative features of a work include such things as its balance, harmoniousness, and strength, for these are based upon our assessment of the work.

The presence of any specific set of descriptive properties does not necessarily make a work better. To see this, consider the claim made by the judge that her initial valuation of Emily's painting was due, in part, to its detail. Can we take the presence of detail to augment the artistic value of a work, so that the absence of detail would then function to the work's detriment?

There are problems with both aspects of this claim. First, while there are works of art whose artistic value stems at least in part from their exquisite detail – I think here of Durer's etchings – too much detail can mar a work.

We would then say the work was fussy or excessively detailed, moving from a description to an evaluation. It's hard to give examples of an excessively detailed painting, since they are not viewed as great paintings. However, you might take a look at *Juggling Dog in Hula Skirt* by Mari Newman in the online *Museum of Bad Art* for one possible example.

Second, there are some works that eschew detail and that we value for their boldness, the presence of broad gestures that depend upon the absence of detail. Works by some of the Abstract Expressionists, like Franz Kline, are like this. Kline's paintings consist of large panels with a few very broad brushstrokes of black paint. Such works have no detail at all, but it's that very fact that contributes to their being the great works that they are.

We now seem to be digging ourselves into an ever-deeper hole in our attempt to explain the rationale behind our evaluative claims about works of art. Although we were very clear that the judge of the first-grade art contest made a mistake in rejecting her initial evaluation of Emily's painting, we have found it more difficult to explain our rationale for making assessments of the merit of works of art.

We can begin to resolve this puzzle by acknowledging that our evaluations of works of art are based in part on our preferences. This is because there is some similarity between saying "The *Mona Lisa* is one of the greatest paintings in the Western tradition," and saying "I love chocolate," for both judgments express our preferences. If I think that the *Mona Lisa* is great, it's in part because I get pleasure from looking at it, just as my love of chocolate is based upon the pleasure eating it gives me.

However, there are significant differences between these two judgments as well. When I say that I love chocolate, the amount of pleasure I get when I eat it justifies the claim. If you say you don't like chocolate, I can't rationally argue with you. How could I even start? If I said, "Chocolate tastes so good!", you would just reassert your disagreement with what I've said. Significantly, there is nothing that I could say to make you change your mind. I like one flavor; you like another. End of story.

Not so with the *Mona Lisa*. If I tell you that it is among the greatest paintings ever painted and you say you don't really like it, that does not end our conversation. In fact, it's more likely to initiate a long discussion. I might call up an image of the painting on the internet and point out the woman's enigmatic smile, the pyramidal structure of her body, and so on. In doing this, I act on my belief that my evaluation of this work (and, indeed, all artworks) is not *just* an expression of my personal taste. I think that there is something in the painting itself that you will be able to see if you will only take the trouble to look at it carefully, given my advice.

But this means that my "taste" in paintings is not like my preference for one flavor of ice-cream over another. When Emily thought that artistic evaluations were similar to gustatory ones, she was simply mistaken.

You still might not be convinced of this claim. After all, some people like Impressionist landscapes and others prefer Abstract Expressionist canvases. Am I really claiming that a judgment like "Monet's *Impression Sunrise* is a better painting than Franz Kline's *High Street*" has an objective basis? It seems hard to think of empirical evidence – other than one's experience of the paintings – that could serve to justify this evaluative claim.

One possible attempt at a way out of this dilemma is to consider the artistic value of a work of art relative to the goals that were targeted in creating it. One would then claim that, relative to a given goal, an artistic evaluation was objective.

In fact, this provides us with a way of accounting for our sense that Emily's paintings are quite remarkable. Emily is clearly trying to create paintings that convey an idea she has about the subject of her painting. Because she thinks Ms Fair is wonderful, she paints her with angel's wings. In so doing, she adds an element to her depiction of Ms Fair that moves the painting beyond the realm of pure representation: the angel's wings in this painting, the large ears in Thor's case. And when we judge the painting of Thor to be good, we are saying both that Emily achieved her goal and that she did so in a way that we appreciate, especially in someone so young.

This suggestion does not fully resolve our perplexity about artistic evaluations, though, for it does not provide us with a standard that will work across all types of art. Sure, Emily's painting realizes her expressive intentions quite well. But are her paintings better than some other first-graders' paintings that are successful in terms of the accuracy of their representation of their objects? There still is no single standard by means of which we can assess the artistic value of all works of art.

Here is a different suggestion about a standard for artistic evaluation. Think back to that list of the 10 greatest composers of all time. One feature that was necessary for a composer to appear on the list was their *originality*. A composer who just followed the model set up by previous composers would not be considered really great, even if their music was very pleasant to listen to. Originality is an important fact about works of art as well as artists, one that is necessary for both of them to be judged truly great.

In saying this, I am not claiming that everyone values originality equally. Nonetheless, a painting that exhibits originality will be a better painting than one with virtually identical descriptive features that lacks it, as the example of Kelly's butterflies makes clear. Kelly's paintings do not exhibit originality because she just follows a simple pattern that Emily taught her, and that makes her paintings less artistically valuable, less good. Emily, on the other hand, exhibits great originality in her work and that is a partial explanation of our sense that her paintings are good, indeed much better than Kelly's.

Consideration of originality as a criterion for evaluating the merit of paintings shows us a crucial difference between our judgments about ice-cream flavors and our artistic evaluations. While my preference for chocolate ice-cream is justified simply by how it tastes, the originality of a work of art is not something I directly perceive. When I look at one of Monet's *Water Lily* paintings and am struck by its originality, I am not basing my evaluation solely on the painting I am looking at. The originality of this work has to do with its relation to paintings by Monet's predecessors and contemporaries. I might be referring, for example, to the way in which Monet revolutionizes his predecessors' use of the canvas to represent a three-dimensional scene. But for me to be right about this, I need to know at least something about art history and Monet's position within it. My judgment and my appreciation of Monet are thus based on more than the sensory pleasure that I experience when I look at *Water Lilies* in the Museum of Modern Art in New York. And that's simply not the case when I eat a chocolate bar. My evaluation of it is based completely on the pleasure I get from eating it.

At least some of our confusion about artistic evaluation is cleared up with the recognition that originality is a necessary condition for a work being valuable. It also shows us that judgments about the artistic value of works of art are not simply based upon our individual, subjective reactions to the works. There are objective facts about the works, including their originality, that are the basis for our artistic evaluation of them.

But what about Emily? We left her after the judge had changed her mind about her painting of Thor and given the prize to her best friend instead. This prompts a serious crisis for Emily and for her friendship with Kelly. After a difficult time, the two of them reconcile and Emily takes back her decision never to paint again. A tragedy has been averted. Emily returns to her pursuit of painting, despite her frustration over the outcome of what may have been a very ill-conceived first-grade art contest.

Our examination of the judge's decision in the art contest has led us to an investigation of the standards we use in judging works of art. We have not considered what makes her decision *unfair*. To do so would be to enter the realm of ethics, the subject of the next chapter.

Discussing the Philosophy of Art with Children

Art is a subject that interests children because they often are engaged in producing it. So an interesting way to begin a discussion of issues in the philosophy of art is to ask the children whether they prefer Kelly's paintings or Emily's and why. Once they explain, ask them whether they think that other people should agree with them, or if it's fine for other people to disagree. And, as usual, ask them to explain why they think what they think.

10

Miss Nelson Is Missing!

Is It Okay for Adults to Deceive Kids?

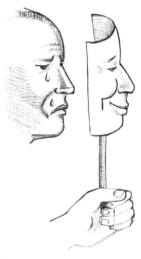

Is it okay for adults to deceive kids?

Harry Allard's very engaging and popular picture book *Miss Nelson Is Missing!* raises an important ethical issue: Does the end justify the means? This is a question that you have probably heard people ask, and it is a good place to begin our study of ethics. The issue is whether it is morally permissible to adopt an immoral means if doing so promotes a morally good end.

In the book, Miss Nelson, a very nice but ineffectual teacher, resorts to deception to get her students to behave. As the story opens, she is having terrible trouble controlling the students in her elementary school classroom. The children constantly misbehave and don't listen to her when she tries to get them to stop. Even during the much-valued read-aloud, the kids keep up their antics. Something has to be done.

A Sneetch Is a Sneetch and Other Philosophical Discoveries: Finding Wisdom in Children's Literature, First Edition. Thomas E. Wartenberg. Illustrations © Joy Kinigstein.
© 2013 John Wiley & Sons, Inc. Published 2013 by John Wiley & Sons, Inc.

The next day, a substitute teacher appears. It is Miss Viola Swamp. Miss Swamp is everything Miss Nelson is not: She's ugly, while Miss Nelson is beautiful; she wears black, Miss Nelson, pink; her hair is black, Miss Nelson's, blonde. She is a witch, the students conclude, and she means business. She loads the children down with homework and cancels the read-aloud, keeping them in line with her tough and threatening manner.

The children are so upset they even hire a detective to try and locate Miss Nelson. Then, they take matters into their own hands and go to Miss Nelson's house to find her. When they see Miss Viola Swamp coming down the street, they flee in fear. They imagine all sorts of fates to have befallen Miss Nelson. Are they doomed to have Miss Viola Swamp as their teacher forever?

Fortunately not. They are saved when the lovely Miss Nelson suddenly reappears one day. But how things have changed in the classroom! The children now behave so well they don't even misbehave during the read-aloud. Miss Nelson's unruly students have become models of diligence and respect.

When Miss Nelson goes home from school that afternoon, she hangs her lovely dress next to an ugly black one, revealing what we had already surmised: that she had masqueraded as Miss Viola Swamp. Clearly, she had created this deception in order to get her students to behave better.

Miss Nelson Is Missing! is a very charming book. The illustrations are simple but evocative. The story is told with wit and humor. And we take pleasure in our ability to solve the riddle of Miss Viola Swamp while the children remain deceived by Miss Nelson's clever stratagem.

Miss Nelson's ruse of pretending to be Miss Viola Sharp is extremely effective in getting the children to behave, something that continues when Miss Nelson herself returns to the classroom. But in solving the behavior problem in her classroom, she deceives the children. This raises the ethical question of whether her deception of the children, no matter how well intentioned, is morally wrong. Can something that is inherently morally wrong, like deceiving others, become morally acceptable if the deception is pursued for a good purpose, as it is when Miss Nelson deceives the children? Can the worthiness of her goal justify the employment of the morally dubious means she employs?

Ethics

Ethics focuses on the question of how human beings should live their lives. Some examples of ethical questions are: Is it permissible for people in the United States to buy luxury goods when the money they spend could save the lives of starving people in other countries? And, is it morally permissible to kill one innocent person if doing so would spare the lives of many others?

There are three basic approaches to ethics. The first – called *deontology* by philosophers although I will use the less forbidding terminology of *respect* theory – originated in the writings of **Immanuel Kant**, and attempts to justify moral rules, such as "Killing is wrong." On this view, being moral requires you to treat all human beings as *ends* rather than *means*. You treat other people as a means, when you use them to further your own goals, as when you ask someone to pass the salt. Treating another person as an end requires that you respect their desires in deciding what you should do, as when you decide not to steal their wallet because they need the money it contains for their own pursuits.

Utilitarianism takes the promotion of human well-being and the avoidance of suffering to be basic. Utilitarians approve of actions or policies that enhance human well-being more than any available alternative. **Jeremy Bentham** and **John Stuart Mill** are two of the most important classical utilitarians. Because utilitarianism assesses the moral worth of actions by assessing their consequences, it is a form of *consequentialism*.

Virtue ethics takes the goal of ethics to be the articulation of a set of character traits that human beings ought to possess to lead a fulfilling life. Virtue ethics originated in **Aristotle**'s contention that the true subject matter of ethics was how human beings could live a fulfilling life.

You may be puzzled about whether there is a distinction between ethics and morality. Although some philosophers, such as **G.W.F. Hegel**, made a systematic distinction between the two, most philosophers use the two terms interchangeably. I follow that practice here.

In defending her actions, Miss Nelson need not adopt a broad justification of deception. She could argue that there are certain circumstances, such as, perhaps, students continually misbehaving in a classroom, when it is morally permissible to deceive them. The reason is that such deception is necessary in order to get the students to behave better. The assumption is that a short-term morally suspect policy that has huge positive benefits is one that it is permissible to adopt.

This is exactly the reason why Miss Nelson decides to deceive her students. In order to be an effective teacher, she needs to maintain order in her classroom. But she is so nice and friendly with her students that they take advantage of her and don't listen to her when she tries to get them to behave. Since she cannot teach effectively in her unruly classroom, she needs to figure out a way of maintaining control and getting the students to behave. But how can she do that when she has tried everything and nothing has worked?

It is in these straits that Miss Nelson decides to rely on deception. Our question, though, is not about the effectiveness of her stratagem, but about its morality.

Philosophers of a Kantian bent would argue that it is always wrong to deceive someone. Do you agree?

In order to investigate this question, you need to realize that, when you deceive someone, you are not being truthful with them. Deception is similar to, but also different from, lying. Miss Nelson doesn't explicitly lie to her students, but she certainly is not always truthful with them.

We therefore find ourselves having to answer this more fundamental question: What makes telling the truth morally right and not telling it morally wrong?

Here is a sketch of a justification of the principle, "Always tell the truth": It is important for people to tell others the truth because everyone will be better off living in a society in which people normally are truthful. Why? Because only if people can ordinarily be relied upon to tell the truth, will you have a reason to *trust* them and trust is one of the most important features of society.

Think about it. If people couldn't trust others to tell them the truth, life would be difficult, much more difficult in fact than it is now. For example, when you go to the store to buy something, you trust that the grocer is giving you what you asked for. When she weighs the vegetables you want, you expect that she is telling you what they actually weigh. And similar things hold for virtually all of your social interactions with other people: You usually trust what people say to you because you act under the presumption that people generally tell the truth.

A society in which you couldn't trust others to tell the truth would be pervaded by suspicion and fear. Imagine what it would be like if you couldn't trust the gas station pump to accurately measure the actual number of gallons you pump into your car's tank. You certainly would be suspicious and try to figure out a way to gauge the accuracy of the pump on your own. But how would you go about doing this? It's not immediately apparent, and that's one of the reasons why pumps are regularly inspected by the government to insure their accuracy. In our hypothetical non-truth telling society, though, you would also have no reason to trust the government. Fear, suspicion, and anxiety would become widespread and endemic.

Thomas Hobbes famously described this situation as *a state of nature* and he characterized life in it as "solitary, poor, nasty, brutal, and short." It's the reason he thought that people would agree to be subject to a central political authority.

Clearly, you are much better off living in a society in which you can generally trust people to be truthful. Although our society does not uniformly realize this ideal, truthfulness remains an ideal that we expect our institutions to live up to.

The type of reasoning I have just employed is an example of a *consequentialist* justification of an ethical norm or rule. As the terms suggests, a consequentialist assesses the *consequences* of various alternative actions or policies, and adopts the one with the best overall results. My argument in favor of telling the truth depends on comparing a society with truth tellers to one populated by deceivers. I argue that a society in which people tell the truth is better because it produces the highest level of welfare possible. As a result, the moral rule "Always tell the truth!" is justified.

Many philosophers reject a consequentialist justification of moral rules. For them, we should tell the truth because doing so respects the person to whom we tell it, while deceiving them or lying to them does not. Philosophers of the ilk – *respect theorists* – take respect for others to be so basic to human social interaction that it can be used as the basis for assessing the morality of our actions.

Although consequentialists and respect theorists disagree on why it's wrong to lie, they both agree that telling the truth is a fundamental moral rule. So let's consider a slight different issue: Are there ever circumstances in which it is legitimate to allow exceptions to the policy or moral rule, "Always tell the truth"?

This question brings to the fore one feature of moral rules that we have not yet discussed explicitly, namely that they always have what I call an *escape clause*. An escape clause comes at the end of a moral rule or policy like "Always tell the truth!" And what it says is "unless there are special circumstances." When those special circumstances apply, the policy or rule no longer applies.

What's an example of an escape clause to a moral rule? Think about the moral rule against killing. This moral rule goes all the way backed to the Ten Commandments in the Bible and many people accept it as a valid moral rule. But when they do, they almost always think of it as implicitly having an escape clause. For example, most people believe it is all right to kill an enemy soldier in wartime or even, in non-wartime, to kill when one does so in self-defense. Wartime and self-defense are examples of the special circumstances in which the escape clause to the moral rule against killing is triggered.

Clearly, only certain, very special circumstances can be included in the escape clause of any moral rule or else the rule itself would be meaningless. If you could claim that there were special circumstances anytime you wanted to tell a lie, then the moral rule against lying would be worthless. You could violate it at will and then justify the morality of your action by saying, "But don't you see, there were special circumstances and that's why it was morally all right for me to lie."

What's necessary, then, is a way of specifying which circumstances are to count as legitimate exceptions to a moral rule. One reason we allow an exception to a moral rule is that there is a competing, more significant rule that also applies. Consider the exception to the rule for killing in cases of self-defense. Why is all right to kill someone in self-defense, i.e., when they are threatening your life? Because we have a moral right to defend ourselves when our life is threatened. In extreme circumstances – such as when someone is threatening to kill you and the only way for you to save your life is to kill them – your moral right to defend your own life takes precedence over the moral rule not to kill another person or, in other words, the escape clause to the moral rule against killing applies.

This discussion of moral rules and escape clauses provides us with the resources necessary for determining whether it was morally permissible for Miss Nelson to deceive her students. To answer this question, let's start by thinking about why it is generally wrong to deceive someone about something.

One reason why deception is wrong is that it is contrary to the policy of telling the truth. So the general justification we considered in favor of telling the truth makes it wrong to deceive someone. That's why Miss Nelson does something morally wrong in deceiving the children, even though her doing so had some significant positive effects.

There are various ways in which you might argue that Miss Nelson did not really do something morally objectionable. You might deny that deception runs afoul of our obligation to tell the truth. A lie, on this view, is an explicit statement a person makes that he knows not to be true. So I lie to you when you ask me whether I will visit my mother this week and I say, "Yes," knowing that I have no intention to. Clearly, in this case I have not told you the truth. But if you tell me that you assume I'll be visiting my mother and I don't do anything to correct your mistaken belief, I may be deceiving you but I'm not lying.

The issue here has to do with the scope of our moral obligation to tell the truth. Does it entail that we have an obligation to correct people's misapprehensions as well as to directly tell them the truth? I think it does, at least if we are responsible for their misapprehension, so that deception is wrong because it violates our obligation to tell the truth.

That's why it won't do to say that Miss Nelson was not really lying, so that there was nothing immoral in pretending to be Miss Viola Swamp. While it's true that she didn't explicitly lie to the children about who Miss Viola Swamp was, she did know that they were very upset that she, Miss Nelson, was missing, and she did nothing to correct their mistaken impression that she was not Miss Viola Swamp. She knowingly and intentionally misled them, and that is something that the obligation to tell the truth prohibits as immoral.

Nor can you say that there is an escape clause to Miss Nelson's obligation to tell her students the truth that justifies her deception. As I indicated earlier, in order for the escape clause to apply, there would need to be a moral rule to take precedence over the moral rule not to deceive. Although there certainly are circumstances in which it is morally permissible to deceive someone – think here of deceiving a mafia hit man who asks you for directions to the house of the person he intends to kill – Miss Nelson is not in a situation like that. Having to manage an unruly classroom does not constitute a situation in which the general obligation to be truthful in one's dealings with others no longer applies.

But this does point the way to a type of justification often given for not telling the truth: that one is telling the lie for the good of the person being lied to. The general term for such lies is *white lie*, and the usual justification for telling them is that they are told for the benefit of the person being lied to.

Consider, for example, a deathbed lie. Say that a good friend of yours is about to die and he asks you whether you mailed the letter he gave you for his estranged brother. Assume that you forgot, but that you can easily mail the letter later in the day. You have a choice: you could tell your dying friend the truth, and cause him a great deal of anguish, let us assume, or you could tell him a lie and he will then die contented, knowing that his last letter has been mailed. The general rationale for lying in this and similar cases – one favored by consequentialists – is that lying in these circumstances has no negative effects. In the case I described, your friend will soon be dead, so he won't have a chance to discover that you have lied, and you will be making his last moments much more pleasant by telling a harmless lie.

This issue of deathbed lie opens up a very large topic in medical ethics, a field in which ethical considerations are applied to a wide range of medical issues. There is a lot of disagreement about whether physicians have an obligation to tell their patients the truth about their condition, for example, even when doing so might create a problem in their treatment. But rather than wade more deeply into those interesting waters, I want to return to *Miss Nelson Is Missing!* Can we justify what she did on the grounds that it, like a white lie, was told for the benefit of those to whom she lied?

I would imagine that Miss Nelson, if she actually existed, would appeal to something like that. The reason she cooked up her deceit, I suspect she would say, was that she wanted to find a way to teach the children how to behave that didn't jeopardize her relationship with them. She invented the Miss Viola Sharp ruse to get the children to change their behavior and that is what justifies making an exception to the general moral rule that it is wrong to deceive people in this case.

A fairly obvious response to Miss Nelson's hypothetical self-defense is that she underestimates the harm that might come from the children believing her masquerade. There is always the chance that they will discover what she has done, and then be even less willing to listen to her than they were before she adopted it. They would also feel aggrieved if they find out that their beloved teacher had deceived them.

But even if her ruse remained undiscovered, there is reason to believe that she acted immorally, for she treated the children in a way that we would not want them to treat others, one that did not *respect* them. Especially in an educational setting, an adult should behave in the way we expect children to. And Miss Nelson's policy of deception is not something that we would like to see the children adopt in their dealings with others.

Miss Nelson Is Missing! presents a story that we need to heed as a warning. It shows us how successful deceptive behavior can be and also provides us with an opportunity for reflecting on why such behavior is morally wrong.

So there is a lesson to be learned about the importance of approaching children's picture books armed with philosophy. If a parent just reads *Miss Nelson Is Missing!* to a child without raising the issue of whether what Miss Nelson did was moral, the child might come away thinking that her parent approved of Miss Nelson's actions. And, if the child took this to heart, she might think that it was all right to deceive others so long as one did so for their own benefit. Additionally, this child would have a reason not to trust adults, for they would have shown her that they thought that deceiving children was not always morally wrong.

In this case, then, we don't just learn some philosophy from reading a children's picture book. Rather, by using the book as an occasion for philosophical reflection on the morality of deception, we find ourselves not only engaging more fully with the book and its narrative, but also creating an opportunity to reassure our children about our relationship with them.

Discussing the Morality of Deception with Children

Is it ever morally right to deceive someone? This is the question you might raise in your discussion. You can do so by first asking whether it is right for Miss Nelson to deceive her class and why. Assuming that the children say no, you could ask them if they ever think it is all right to deceive someone. Keep in mind the deathbed lie as an example of a lie that might be morally permissible. Are there others?

11

The Giving Tree

How Can It Be Wrong to Give Someone What They Want?

How can it be wrong to give someone what they want?

Shel Silverstein's *The Giving Tree* is a favorite of many children, adults, and teachers. The story of a relationship between a boy and a tree is charming for, despite the vicissitudes of the relationship, the two end up together at the end, with the boy – now an old man – sitting contentedly on the tree – itself reduced to a mere stump.

The book raises an important issue in the field of *environmental ethics*. As the name indicates, environmental ethics applies our general ethical views to the specific case of our treatment of the natural world, our environment. It will be a fitting continuation of our discussion of picture-book ethics, for we will see that the somewhat abstract considerations I raised concerning morality in the last chapter acquire a new significance and concreteness when applied to issues about the appropriate relationship of humans to the non-human entities that surround them.

A Sneetch Is a Sneetch and Other Philosophical Discoveries: Finding Wisdom in Children's Literature,
First Edition. Thomas E. Wartenberg. Illustrations © Joy Kinigstein.
© 2013 John Wiley & Sons, Inc. Published 2013 by John Wiley & Sons, Inc.

Environmental Ethics

Human actions are drastically affecting the earth, with severe weather patterns becoming more common and global warming now accepted by virtually the entire scientific community. *Environmental ethics* has become increasingly significant, as the need to address global environmental issues becomes urgent and unavoidable.

Environmental ethics is one field of *applied ethics*, which also includes bio-medical ethics and business ethics. Each of these fields applies general ethical principles to its specific area of concern. The topics of euthanasia and abortion are examples of issues discussed in bio-medical ethics while the topics of whistle-blowers and managerial salaries are two of those addressed by business ethics.

Environmental ethics raises various issues about the relationship between human beings and their natural environment. These include:

- Is it morally permissible to eat animals?
- Is species variety an important value that should be promoted for its own sake?
- Do trees and other forms of plant life have a right to exist?
- Should companies be held responsible for the environmental degradation they cause?
- What constitutes just reparation for environmental damage?

Environmental ethicists apply the general ethical theories we discussed in chapter 10 to the natural world. Utilitarians argue that enlarging the scope of those considered in utilitarian calculations will change our environmental policies. Simply taking future generations into account, for example, results in greater care being exercised to preserve the natural world for their enjoyment.

Respect theories also seek to enlarge the community of their moral deliberations. They assert, for example, that animals as well as human beings deserve to be treated with respect. This allows them to condemn large-scale factory farming of animals for failing to treat animals respectfully.

But some ecological ethicists criticize more traditional ethical views as being illicitly *anthropocentric*, that is, concentrating on the welfare of human beings at the expense of all other living things. *Deep ecologists* articulate a way of thinking that puts environmental concerns at the center of ethics. They argue, for example, that all living things form a great web, so that any action affects everything.

The Giving Tree presents a series of episodes in which a boy interactions with a tree beginning when the boy is a child and ending when he has become an old man. In the first episode, we see a young boy playing on a tree and are told that the tree enjoys how the boy uses its stout limbs and plentiful leaves, its shade, and its apples. The book states that the boy loved the tree and that, as a result, the tree, which also loved the boy, was happy.

In the next episode, the boy is a teenager and, as such, has other interests besides swinging in a tree. Girls, for instance. So he spends less time with the tree and only visits it to see if it can help him get some money. The tree complies by offering the boy all of its apples, which the boy harvests and sells.

Although this episode ends with a repetition of the earlier refrain, "And the tree was happy," we can see that there has been a fundamental shift in the boy's relationship with the tree. As a young child, the boy and the tree had a relationship characterized by mutual respect, one in which each was concerned with the well-being of the other and enjoyed the other's presence. Although the boy "used" the tree for his own pleasure – climbing its trunk, swinging on its branches, lying in the shade it provided – he did so in a way that didn't harm the tree at all. Their relationship at this point was clearly unproblematic from a moral point of view, not only because both of them were satisfied by it, but because their mutual love and respect made their relationship a paradigm of a morally good one.

Once the boy becomes a teenager, he no longer maintains that type of relationship with the tree, for he only visits it to see if it can be useful to him. Although there is nothing morally problematic in the boy's relationship with the tree at this stage – after all, gathering and selling the tree's apples does not harm the tree in any way – we can already see some signs that the boy's relationship with the tree is becoming exploitative, for he is only interested in what the tree can provide him. No longer does he act respectfully towards the tree, but uses the tree as a means of getting what he wants for himself.

Before developing our ethical analysis of the morality of the boy's actions, we need to continue following the book's narrative, for things get worse for the tree before they get better (if they ever really do). Once he has become a young man, the boy – I will continue to refer to him that way since the book does – stays away for increasingly longer periods of time and the tree becomes sad. The boy returns only to get help from the tree with building a house for his wife and children. The tree, ever willing to give what it has to the boy, offers him its branches for a house. The boy willingly takes these, leaving the tree just a trunk. Nonetheless, this episode still ends with the refrain, "And the tree was happy."

Not so after the boy's next visit. When the boy returns after a very long absence, the tree once again expects the boy to play as he did when he was young. But the boy, now a middle-aged man, is depressed, perhaps because his life has not turned out as he had expected when he optimistically talked to the tree about providing for a wife and children. Once again, the motive for his visit is to get assistance from the tree. This time, the boy wants a boat with which to sail far away, presumably to distance himself from the mess he has made of his life. So the tree – who has by now more than earned the name of the *giving* tree – offers the boy his trunk, and the boy – ever willing to take what the tree offers – cuts down the trunk of the tree, leaving it a mere stump. Finally, the tree exhibits some regret over what the boy has done to it: "And the tree was happy . . . but not really."

At this point in the book, most readers agree that the boy has exploited the tree for his own benefit. Although the tree remains willing to give what it can to help the boy satisfy his burgeoning desires, the tree itself is reduced to nearly nothing. A stump is all that remains.

The concept of exploitation is imbued with a moral evaluation. A relationship is *exploitative* when one of the parties in it takes unfair advantage of the other. Within philosophy, the term was first systematically used by **Karl Marx** who argued that the capitalist economic system was based on the exploitation of workers by owners. More recently, environmental ethicists have applied the term to the relationship of human beings to the natural world.

When we say that humans are exploiting the natural world, we are presuming that there is something *unfair* or immoral about the way in which human beings are treating nature. This claim extends ethical relationships beyond the human realm, whereas philosophers in the Western tradition had generally limited their moral concerns to relationships between human beings. So, for example, **Immanuel Kant**, the founder of respect theory discussed in the last chapter, assumed that the only beings worthy of respect were human beings, for only they were capable of acting morally.

Environmental ethicists, on the other hand, have sought to provide a moral framework that takes seriously the fact that human beings are part of a larger natural world. Some of them have simply extended the notion of morally significant entities from human to non-human things, including animals, vegetables, and even rocks. From their point of view, Western ethical views were illicitly *speciesist* when they illegitimately treated members of the species *homo sapiens* – that is, human beings – as the only creatures whose interests mattered from a moral point of view.

This charge applies very clearly to utilitarianism, another of the ethical theories I discussed in the last chapter. The principle of utility states that an action is ethical only if it, more than any available alternative, maximizes the well-being of all those concerned. But in applying that principle, utilitarians simply assumed that the only beings whose well-being mattered were humans. In fact, this assumption is belied by the effects of many of our actions and policies.

Think about the construction of a dam to control flooding and provide electricity. Clearly, there are utilitarian justifications available for such actions so long as more people are helped by such projects than are harmed by them. But there are many creatures affected by a dam in addition to human beings. Many plants and trees will be destroyed, and fish and land animals will likely be displaced or killed. Environmental ethicists argue that we need to take other, non-human beings into account in our determination of whether a particular project is justified or not.

But how are we to compare the welfare of a human being to that of, say, a snail darter, the small fish that acquired notoriety when a large-scale dam project was halted because the darter's existence was threatened? It's not easy to determine how to make such a comparison, and that is why some environmental ethicists have argued that non-human creatures like the snail darter have as much *right to exist*, as do human beings. From their point of view, there is no need to compare the welfare of the inhabitants of a city with the welfare of a biological species, for all biological creatures have an equal right to exist. And, in so doing, they reject a consequentialist framework for ethics in favor of a respect or rights-based view.

But it is not only non-human beings whose existence environmental ethicists push us to acknowledge. For example, consider the question of whether to create national parks. This is a fraught issue because land that was previously available for a variety of human pursuits is preserved from further development, and is hence off-limits for these traditional pursuits. The justification of such a designation is a significant issue, for many people are affected when national parks are created.

Among those most directly affected are those who have traditionally had access to the land. In many cases, there are native peoples who use the land to be designated as a national park for a variety of pursuits, with fishing, hunting, and acquiring wood for heat being paramount. When we designate an area off-limits to such activities, these are the first people to be affected.

Since these people are generally made less well off by the protection of these areas from traditional uses, there needs to be some justification for so doing. Usually, the argument proposes that areas that have not yet been developed should remain pristine so that they will be available to lots of people. But what about those people whose traditional way of life is thereby threatened? Shouldn't they be allowed to pursue their lives in the way that they always have, even if it causes inconvenience for those who want to protect the environment from further degradation?

In order to justify such a claim, environmental ethicists have often made wide-ranging criticisms of the way in which Western philosophy has conceptualized ethical issues. One type of criticism asserts that the entire tradition of Western philosophy has operated with a series of problematic *dichotomies* that illicitly promote one term while devaluing the other. Among the objectionable dichotomies are: human versus nature; mind versus body; male versus female; thought versus emotion; and human versus animal. In each of these pairings, the first term is treated as superior to the second, denigrated term. But critics of the role that such dichotomies have played in Western thought think that this is illicit. The supposedly inferior term, they claim, is just as valuable and important as the supposedly superior one. On this view, the Western tradition needs to reconstruct itself in such a way as to acknowledge the value of what it has illicitly denigrated.

Deconstruction

Deconstruction is an approach to interpreting philosophical texts that was developed by the French philosopher **Jacques Derrida**. Derrida thought that Western philosophy was based upon an inadequate metaphysical framework that interpreted reality in light of a variety of hierarchical dichotomies. Beginning with the contrast between written and spoken language, Derrida attempted to show how philosophers had treated one term in a dichotomy – here, speech – as superior to the other – here, writing. Derrida's claim was that whichever term was treated as inferior would reappear in a text in a way that contradicted its denigration.

Derrida's approach to the texts of Western philosophy had a huge impact, not only on philosophy, but also on the humanities more generally. Literary scholars now regularly investigate the "binaries" structuring literary texts. But the impact of deconstruction is not limited to academic settings. People now often speak of "deconstructing an argument" without being aware of the technical meaning of the term, thereby paying witness to the influence of this philosophical movement.

In its broadest sense, deconstruction asks us to pay attention to the unstated presumptions that any philosophical view has. Every view must take something for granted, and it is this unacknowledged basis for our ways of thinking and acting that deconstruction focuses on. In this respect, it is similar to *psychoanalysis*, which deals with unconscious rather than conscious thoughts. Both endeavors seek to make the unacknowledged or unconscious an object of our awareness in order to change our habitual ways of thinking and acting.

Examples of opponents of this *dualistic* mode of thinking are not hard to find. Consider feminists. (We will consider feminist philosophy in more detail in chapter 15.) They assert that, in thinking about gender, Western philosophers have simply assumed without adequate justification that maleness is better than or superior to femaleness. But both men and women are equally capable of rational thought, for example, something the tradition has taken to be the exclusive province of the male half of the species.

Environmental ethicists have applied this critical assessment of the Western, dualistic manner of thinking to develop a more unified conception of existence that does not privilege the human being over other types of beings. Some have asserted that all things are interdependent, so that it is a mistake to see one type of being as superior to another. Others have insisted that all existing things have value, so that humans cannot be segregated as the only bearers of value in the world.

If we look over the history of Western ethical thought, we can see how deeply it is implicated in problematic assumptions about the human–nature relationship. The founding text of the Judeo-Christian tradition, the Bible, asserts that human beings have the right to use nature for their own benefit. *Genesis* (1:26) makes this explicit: "And God said, Let us make man in our image, after our likeness: and let them have dominion over the fish of the sea, and over the fowl of the air, and over the cattle, and over all the earth, and over every creeping thing that creepeth upon the earth." God here appoints human beings as rulers over all of nature – animal, mineral, and vegetable. As such, humans have the right to do with nature what they will.

During the twentieth century, philosophers recognized that human beings could not treat the natural world as something that was simply their dominion, something that they could use as they saw fit. The philosopher, **Martin Heidegger**, for example, proposed that we replace the idea of humans as *rulers* over the natural world with the idea that humans should be *caretakers* of it. Heidegger replaced the hierarchical view of humans as superior to nature with a more egalitarian and reciprocal notion of humans as immersed in and dependent upon the natural world.

Using some of Heidegger's ideas, a distinctive view of the human–nature relationship called *deep ecology* was developed. Deep ecology is critical of those forms of environmental ethics that do not address the relationship between human beings and natural things in a sufficiently fundamental manner. It is not enough, deep ecologists claim, to simply add another set of beings into our utilitarian calculations. Instead, a fundamentally new conception of the human–nature relationship needs to be adopted that recognizes an all-inclusive web of life whose "nodes" include both human and non-human beings. Such an approach undercuts the Western bias that accords greater privilege to the needs and interests of human beings than to those of the non-human world.

Bearing this quick and schematic introduction to environmental ethics in mind, we can now return to *The Giving Tree*. The transformation in how the boy treats the tree as he grows old takes on a new significance in light of the claims of environmental ethics. We now recognize that the boy has an increasingly exploitative relationship with the tree that parallels that of Western society with the natural world in general.

Consider the now middle-aged boy's request that the tree provide him with a boat. Although he doesn't directly ask the tree to allow him to cut down its trunk, that's the only way for the tree to satisfy the boy's desire. At this stage, the boy embodies the problematic assumption that we have seen dominant in Western thinking about natural things like the tree: that they exist solely to satisfy human needs. The book shows the problems with such a way of treating a natural thing by admitting that the "de-trunked" tree no longer felt happy, despite once again sacrificing itself for the boy. Its own being was radically truncated, so to speak, in order to satisfy the boy's needs.

Using the boy's treatment of the tree as a metaphor for the way that Westerners have treated nature, its shortsightedness emerges clearly. For one thing, although the boy-who-has-become-a-man no longer is able to climb up the tree and swing on its limbs, cutting down the tree entails that it is no longer able to provide such outlets for the next generation of boys who come along. The boy has treated the tree as his alone, not thinking about how his destructive act will affect the generations that come after him.

This perspective explains why environmental ethicists have argued that we need to take into account another set of beings in our ethical deliberations: future generations of humans. It is apparent that the boy's destruction of the tree – at least if we see it in metaphorical terms – will leave a much diminished earth to his heirs and the following generation.

The book also suggests a reason for the man-who-had-been-a-boy's selfishness: He becomes depressed as he grows old. Although earlier he had used the tree to provide him with the things he had needed in his optimistic sense that life had a great deal to offer, he later returns to the tree depressed, having found that life did not live up to his expectations.

But *The Giving Tree* does not end on this depressing note, with the tree abandoned by the depressed and selfish man-who-had-once-been-a-boy. One of the reasons people enjoy this book so much is that it ends with a reconciliation between the selfish boy and the tree. In its final episode, the boy, now an elderly man, returns to the tree after an absence of many years. At this point, the tree has almost nothing to give the boy, but the boy's desires have become simple enough that, surprisingly, the tree can still satisfy them: All the boy wants is a place to sit and rest, and that is something that the tree, although now reduced to a mere stump, can provide for him. So once again, the boy takes what the tree has to offer, and, once more, the tree is happy.

This optimistic ending to the story, with the boy and tree reunited in an egalitarian and mutually respectful relationship, offers its readers hope. They feel reassured by this ending, for it suggests that in the end, no matter how badly the boy has treated the tree, the two will remain there for each other, in a mutually respectful relationship, even if it is one that is radically transformed from the one that they initially had.

Regardless of what we think about this ending, for anyone concerned with issues in environmental ethics, the book has sounded a serious note. It asks us to recognize that between childhood and old age, people operating within the Western tradition of ethics are not mindful of the value that the non-human beings in their environment have for them as well as for future generations. Harkening to such warnings, environmental ethicists have attempted to raise important issues about our relationship with the other beings that make up our world.

Discussing Environmental Ethics with Children

To initiate a discussion, you might ask if the children think that the boy always treated the tree with respect. You can then move on to a more general discussion about how human beings should treat trees. Is it all right for us to simply cut them down in order to make lumber without paying attention to what purposes they might serve in their natural state? Should we be concerned with the state in which we leave the world for future generations? What role should those yet to be born play in our ethical decision-making?

12

"Cookies"

What Good Is Having Will-Power If You Don't Have Any More Cookies?

Mmmm, cookies; better not eat too many.

Arnold Lobel's delightful amphibians, Frog and Toad, always seem to stumble onto philosophical problems. Whether it's making a list or taking a walk, Frog and Toad can't seem to do anything without bumping into something so curious that we need to do a lot of philosophical thinking before we're satisfied.

Nowhere is this truer than in the story "Cookies," a story about will-power, a concept central to moral psychology. This area of philosophical investigation bridges the fields of ethics and philosophy of mind, developing an account of the mental faculties necessary for moral – and immoral – behavior.

It all starts harmlessly enough. Toad comes over to Frog's house with a freshly baked batch of cookies. They smell so good that the two of them decide to each have one cookie. But the cookies are so delicious that they agree to each eat another. Realizing they are eating too many and that they will get sick if they don't stop, Frog and Toad elect to have one last cookie. But that resolve also falters. So they have a *very* last cookie, only to find themselves tempted once more to break their resolution.

A Sneetch Is a Sneetch and Other Philosophical Discoveries: Finding Wisdom in Children's Literature,
First Edition. Thomas E. Wartenberg. Illustrations © Joy Kinigstein.
© 2013 John Wiley & Sons, Inc. Published 2013 by John Wiley & Sons, Inc.

Moral Psychology

Why do we persist in doing things that we know are wrong? You can be totally convinced that shoplifting is wrong, be aware of the penalties it has, and still find yourself stealing a trifle that you don't really need. This is the sort of issue addressed by *moral psychology.*

Moral psychology integrates ethics with the philosophy of mind. While ethics discusses questions of right and wrong, moral psychology focuses on what gives us the ability to do what's right despite the attractions of morally problematic courses of action.

One of the interesting claims made by moral psychologists is that human beings are not fully rational, and hence do things that wouldn't make sense if they were, like taking the risk of shoplifting. Failures of rationality also occur in less morally fraught situations, such as eating an ice-cream cone even though you are on a diet. Only on a virtue theory approach to morality, can such a failure be seen as a moral one, which is one of the reasons why virtue theory is attractive to many moral philosophers.

There are many other interesting issues in moral psychology. One concerns the possibility of *altruism*, behavior that puts the welfare of others above one's own. Skeptics deny that altruism is possible, for they say that any action you choose to perform satisfies some desire you have. The purported altruist is simply someone who likes doing things for others.

Another issue is *moral luck*. Most philosophers have thought that a person can only be blamed or praised for things over which he has control. Moral luck denies this idea, asserting that we assess the morality of a person's actions using factors they can't control. Think about Gauguin, a man who deserted his wife and children in order to devote himself to painting. Given the success of his paintings, we have a tendency to ignore what we would see as an ethical failing in a person who acted similarly but failed to achieve artistic greatness. If you agree, then you are acknowledging the role of a person's luck in how we assess the morality of their actions.

Frog says he knows what's wrong: they don't have enough will-power. But Toad is not sure. He doesn't know what will-power is. So Frog tells him:

Will-power is not doing something that you really want to do.

Cookies are so tasty; just one more.

And there we have it: a philosophical conundrum, for Frog's definition of will-power appears self-contradictory. If you *really* want to do something, don't you just go ahead and do it? And if you don't, doesn't that just show you didn't *really* want to? If you answered both those questions affirmatively, as I think you must, then you think Frog's notion of will-power doesn't make sense, for you can't not do something you really want to do.

It's a common experience to wish you had more will-power, though what calls forth that desire depends on the psychology of each person. One of you might find peanuts so delicious that she can't stop eating them, even when she can sense a stomachache on the horizon. Another might find buying that shiny new pair of shoes so compelling that he buys them even though he knows he doesn't need more shoes and has resolved numerous times not to buy any. Whatever your specific Achilles' heel is, there are probably some circumstances in which an injection of some more will-power is just what you need.

In Frog and Toad's case, it is fresh-baked cookies that provide the temptation they can't resist. They find the cookies so delicious that the anticipation of eating another overcomes their understanding of the consequence of doing so: getting really sick.

So, Frog and Toad know that they *should not* eat another cookie, and yet they *cannot stop* themselves. That's precisely what the concept of "will-power" is supposed to explain, for it is a psychological capacity whose absence results in a person not being able to restrain their desires. But, as we've seen, when Frog tries to explain what it is, he winds up with a very confusing, if not self-contradictory definition. So let's try to get clearer about this important notion.

Let's start with "will." This is an idea that philosophers have developed to explain our actions. Normally, whenever we do something, it certainly is true that we do what we do because we had a desire to do it. But just because I have a desire for something does not mean that I will act to fulfill that desire. There are many desires that I have – say, for a brand new Lamborghini or a first-class ticket to fly around the world – that I do not act on. But there are many desires that I have – say, for a glass of single malt Scotch before dinner – which I do act on. So we can say, using the terminology introduced in chapter 6, that having a desire is a necessary, but not a sufficient condition for doing something.

Why do I act on one desire – will it – and not on another? At least in some cases, it's because the desire we act on is stronger than the desire you decide not to will. You might, for example, find a new pair of running shoes so desirable that you go out and buy them, but a belt that you also want seems not nearly so enticing, with the result that you don't act on that desire.

In other cases, you might have a strong desire but find the consequences of fulfilling it so detrimental that you choose not to fulfill it. A person may find himself attracted to the spouse of a good friend but not act so as to realize his desire because of the terrible consequences that would ensue if he did.

These are but two explanations for why we act on some desires – *will* them – but not on others. We can see why philosophers would find themselves distinguishing a special mental capacity whose role it is to make the decision to act on certain desires and not on others.

So much for the "will" in will-power, but where does *power* come in? Precisely in situations in which you don't want to satisfy a desire you have. Desires are generally motivating. What this means is that, all other things being equal, if you desire something, you will do what is necessary to satisfy that desire.

If you want *not* to satisfy a desire, you need to have some ability to defeat the motivational push of that desire. It's like having a weight suspended from a pulley that's attached to the ceiling. The weight has a natural tendency to fall because of gravity. If that tendency is to be overcome, there must be some force that is applied in the opposite direction that counteracts the weight's natural tendency. A desire is like the weight in that it pushes to be satisfied and the "power" component of will-power is like the force you exert to keep the weight from falling.

What good is having will-power if you don't have any more cookies?

The concept of will-power is linked to an important philosophical concept, weakness of the will. The Greek philosopher **Aristotle** first identified this phenomenon. For this reason, philosophers often refer to it as *Akrasia*, using the Greek term that Aristotle employed. Aristotle was puzzled by the phenomenon we have just been looking at, albeit mostly in ethical contexts. He wanted to understand how people could know what the appropriate thing to do is but still choose to do something else. His account of *Akrasia* aims to remove the air of paradox from the phenomenon, just as we are doing.

Let's look at a clear example of weakness of the will. Consider Sam, who has gone on a diet and resolved not to eat fattening things. Sam decides to have a cup of black coffee, so he goes into the nearest coffee shop and there, right in front of him, are some freshly baked brownies. Sam has resolved *not* to eat fattening things, but those brownies smell so good and promise so much immediate pleasure. He breaks his resolution and goes ahead and orders a brownie, probably feeling guilty as he wallows in the pleasures provided by that delicious chocolate.

Why does it make sense to talk of *weakness* here? Because the immediate pleasure that Sam believes he will get from doing what he had resolved not to overwhelms his ability to stick to his resolution. It's as if the prospect of the immediate pleasure associated with brownie-eating is so great that it undoes Sam's decision not to eat fattening things. His *will* is too *weak* to overcome the power that the desire for the brownie exerts.

Not all cases of weakness of the will involve immediate pleasure or, for that matter, eating. All that is required is that there be a desire that you are not able to resist satisfying even though you have resolved to resist it. A young guitarist might have resolved to give up the life of a musician because the toll of living on the road was too great, and decided to pursue a PhD in, say, philosophy. But then she gets offered a tour with stops in London, Paris, and Rome, and the lure of those places is just too great. So instead of finishing her dissertation on Aristotle's theory of *Akrasia*, she goes off on tour, knowing that she has succumbed to a weak will.

It's time to get back to Frog and Toad. When we left them, Frog had explained to Toad that their problem was they lacked will-power and he explained that notion as not doing something you really want to do. We have now seen that Frog's explanation makes sense, for someone with will-power will be able to resist the pull of their desires, and that's precisely what he and Toad cannot do.

So what are Frog and Toad to do about those scrumptious cookies, given their lack of will-power? Frog thinks he has a solution. He puts the cookies into a box so that they will not eat them, but Toad points out that they can just open it. So Frog takes a string and ties the box shut. This time, Toad explains that they can untie the string and open the box, giving them access to the cookies. So Frog gets a ladder and puts the cookies way up high on a shelf. Once again, Toad sees a way to defeat Frog's attempt: just climb the ladder and get the cookies down. Finally, in desperation Frog takes the cookies outside and calls out to the neighboring birds. The birds come and make quick work of the remaining cookies, thereby solving Frog and Toad's problem. Or have they?

Toad is distraught. After all, they no longer have any more delicious cookies to eat. Yes, Frog tells him, but what they do have is plenty of will-power. To which Toad responds by telling Frog to keep all of that will-power for himself, he's going home to bake a cake.

This very clever and entertaining end to the story also raises an interesting philosophical question: Is Frog correct when he claims that he and Toad still have will-power after the birds have eaten all the cookies? After all, the temptation has been removed by Frog's final stratagem. Must there be a temptation in order for you to have will-power?

You might think that that neither Frog nor Toad has will-power at the end of the story. After all, you might say, a person can only exercise will-power in the face of a temptation. For example, if you don't like cookies, then you won't be exercising will-power by not eating them even if they smell delicious to you and they are right there in front of you. Only a person who really wants to eat cookies can exercise will-power by deciding not to.

You might have noticed a slight equivocation in the last paragraph. Frog claimed that he and Toad *had* or *possessed* will-power, while I discussed some of the necessary conditions for *exercising* will-power. This is an important distinction. You can agree that neither Frog nor Toad was exercising will-power at the end of the story, because there was no temptation for them to exercise their will-power on, without thereby agreeing that they did not *have* will-power. How can that be?

Let's get Toad out of the way before we answer that question. He never had will-power and therefore didn't exercise any. He appears the complete *hedonist*, someone who is only motivated by a desire for pleasure. What he shows us is that there is something self-defeating in a very simple-minded version of hedonism. If you always choose to pursue that which satisfies your strongest immediate pleasure, you will wind up like Toad probably did, with a bad stomachache from eating too many sweets.

Hedonists do not have to be as irrational as Toad, sating their desires to the point of nausea. A hedonist can be rational, weigh pleasures and pains in such a way as to avoid that fate. The Greek philosopher **Epicurus** developed such a system of rational hedonism that placed the avoidance of pain on an equal footing with the attainment of pleasure.

So, what about Frog? I just explained why he was a bit too generous when he told Toad that *they* had will-power. But was he at least right about himself? I think so. Frog had to have will-power in order to hit upon the various different strategies he used to keep Toad and himself from eating themselves sick. At each stage – when he put the cookies in a box, when he tied a string around the box, when he put the cookies out of their reach, and finally when he gave them to the birds – he was *exercising* will-power. That is, he was trying to prevent himself from exhibiting weakness of the will by eating too many cookies and becoming sick to his stomach.

What makes the story so funny is that every time Frog exercises his will-power Toad figures out a way to circumvent the obstacles Frog places in their way. Though Frog is trying to help them both exercise will-power, the only time he actually exercises his will-power successfully for the *two* of them is when he gives the cookies to the birds, for only then is Toad prohibited from eating any more cookies – although he was able to storm off to bake a cake.

So Frog has will-power and he exercises it a number of times. The odd thing about the end of the book is that the following two claims are true:

1. Throughout the book, Frog has some will-power.
2. At the end of the book, Frog is not exercising any will-power.

The reason that this is not a contradiction is that Frog exercised his will-power *earlier* by getting rid of the very thing whose temptation was so great that he kept falling prey to weakness of the will. What Frog decides to do – very rationally – is to exercise his will-power in such a way that he will not have to keep using it.

In acting in this way, Frog is recognizing some basic features of human – I mean, amphibian – life. Most of us resemble Frog more than we do Toad. That is, there are certain things that we find so tempting that we cannot refrain from acting self-destructively in regard to them. In response, many of us try to increase our will-power so that we won't give in to temptation. I think that **St Augustine** attempts this in his *Confessions* when he prays to God to give him the strength not to do the things he wants to. God can help out here because He provides an external source of strength that Augustine finds lacking in himself. But those stubborn desires keep coming back, so he needs to keep asking God for his help in not giving in to temptation.

Many of us don't turn to God for help in this way. We follow Frog's example instead. We try to keep ourselves, as the expression goes, out of harm's way. We do this by giving our cookies to the birds, metaphorically speaking. We try not to be in situations in which we have to resist the temptation that we know we are not strong enough to resist.

So far, the examples of temptations that I have mentioned have been pretty benign. But there are very serious temptations that most of us have to face, and we need to develop a rational strategy for dealing with them. Consider an alcoholic. How should an alcoholic use his will-power to deal with the temptation that alcohol presents? One way would be to put that bottle of scotch on a table and sit down right in front of it, refusing to take a drink. But given that we are talking about someone who is addicted to alcohol, that would not be a wise course of action, even if it does give him the opportunity to exercise plenty of will-power all of the time. Wiser is the alcoholic who exercises will-power by not putting himself in situations where he will be tempted to drink, such as going to a bar or keeping a ready supply of liquor in his kitchen.

Similar things can be said about many tempting things whose attractions we want to resist. Whenever we think we should not do something that we find very tempting, we would do well to exercise our will-power by keeping ourselves away from opportunities where we are all too likely to give in to the pull of that temptation.

One thing that we can learn from this discussion is that will-power is not simply something that you either have or don't have. For one thing, will-power has to be considered in relation to a particular object or desire. You might not have much will-power when it comes to, say, eating peanuts, but have plenty of will-power when it comes to cleaning your home on a beautiful day that tempts you to take a walk or go for a bike ride.

Perhaps even more importantly, will-power is something that you can have more or less of. Frog certainly has some will-power, for without it he wouldn't have been able to get rid of the cookies. But he also clearly lacks a sufficient amount of will-power to keep himself from eating too many cookies in the first place.

So we can learn some lessons about living our lives in a rational way from Frog and Toad. Although they both are subject to real temptation, Frog pursues a strategy for dealing with it that is admirable and that we would all do well to emulate. He recognizes the limits of his own will-power and acts to extricate himself from a situation in which he will not be able to do what he really wants to. Being aware of what the limits are to his supply of will-power, he exercises it in order to keep himself from being defeated by a temptation that he cannot resist.

Discussing Will-Power with Children

The question of whether Frog and Toad both, or one or neither, possess will-power at the end of the story is a good one to begin a discussion of this interesting philosophical topic with children. You may have to persevere, but they are likely to change their initial assessment if you point out all the things that Frog does to keep the two of them from overeating.

It might also be interesting to go on to ask the children whether they think will-power is an important thing to have. After all, Toad tells Frog that he can keep it as he heads home to bake a cake. Are they more Frog-like or Toad-like? Do they think that's a good thing? Why?

13

Frederick

Can You Enjoy Doing Something Even If It's Work?

Can you enjoy doing something even if it's work?

On a nice fall day, all the members of the mouse family are working hard, gathering corn, nuts, wheat, and straw for the upcoming winter. All, that is, but Frederick.

When his family members ask him why he's not working, Frederick responds by saying that he is gathering sunrays for the cold winter days. As the other mice continue to gather their food, aware that the winter will be long and cold, Frederick remains sitting quietly. In response to their further questions, he tells them he is gathering colors, since there won't be any colors in winter. One day, Frederick seems nearly asleep, but he tells his increasingly annoyed family members that he is actually gathering words so there will be things to talk about during the long winter.

A Sneetch Is a Sneetch and Other Philosophical Discoveries: Finding Wisdom in Children's Literature, First Edition. Thomas E. Wartenberg. Illustrations © Joy Kinigstein.
© 2013 John Wiley & Sons, Inc. Published 2013 by John Wiley & Sons, Inc.

Social and Political Philosophy

Is it fair that some people have much, much more than they need while others are starving? Why do we think that each person should get exactly one vote? Should there be laws against pornography? These are examples of questions that are discussed in *social and political philosophy*.

At the core of this field is the question of what legitimation there is for the existence of society? One school of social and political philosophy treats society as the result of a (hypothetical) *social contract* between the individuals that make it up. But *contractarians* disagree about what limits there should be on the governing authority. Some, like **Thomas Hobbes**, think there are no limits at all on the power of the central authority or *sovereign*. Others, like **John Locke**, think that there is a clear domain in which individuals can legitimately be protected from government intervention.

In the twentieth century, **John Rawls** developed a hugely influential contractarian account of justice. Rawls claimed that justice requires a presumption in favor of equality that can only be violated if the worst-off person benefits from an inequality. Libertarians like **Robert Nozick** objected, claiming that an inequality resulting from freely engaged-in exchanges did not violate presumptions about justice. On the other hand, Marxist philosophers like **Gerald Cohen** argued that even some of the inequalities countenanced by Rawls were illegitimate. More recently, another alternative has been added to the mix, *communitarianism*. Communitarians object to the individualistic bias of contract theory, arguing that there is a more substantive link between individuals and the community of which they are a part.

Social and political philosophers also argue about more specific issues, such as the justification for abortion and the legitimacy of private property. The scope of social and political philosophy is extremely broad, extending to virtually every sphere of human social life.

Leo Lionni's charming tale of a mouse, eponymously named Frederick, raises very important questions about the nature of work, a topic addressed in the field of social and political philosophy. Is Frederick a shirker? If he is, has he forfeited his right to the grain the other mice have collected? Or should he be fed, simply because he is a member of the mouse family? These questions and others like them naturally occur as we ponder this unusual tale.

Although you might be tempted to jump in and answer these questions, I suggest you hold off until you have heard the rest of the story. When winter arrives, the mice all go to their nice hideaway in an abandoned stone wall. At first, their supplies are plentiful and they are all happy, with food to eat and stories with which to entertain each other. But slowly they run out of food and they no longer are so happy and bubbly.

Recalling what Frederick said he was doing while they were gathering food for the winter, his family members turn to him, asking him about his supplies. Frederick responds by asking them to imagine the gold rays of sun and, do you know what? The other mice feel warmer.

Frederick continues by describing all sorts of colorful plants and bushes to his family so that they can envision the colors that faded from view with the coming of winter. He even recites a poem about the different seasons and how they always succeed one another.

When Frederick is done, his family applaud and exclaim that he is a poet. Although Frederick is a bit embarrassed, he acknowledges the truth of what they have said and all the mice are reconciled, for Frederick's poetry has helped his family survive the long, cold winter.

The other mice change their mind about Frederick. At first, they were resentful that Frederick was not sharing the burden of gathering supplies for the winter. But they come to see that he had been gathering his own supplies all along. While it appeared that he had not been doing anything, he really was working, only the character of his work differed from theirs. How can we account for the shift in the other mice's view of Frederick?

It may seem obvious to you what qualifies an activity as work. It's what you get compensated for doing. But things are not that simple. After all, the field mice are engaged in some pretty difficult work when they gather food for the winter, but they are not being paid for their efforts. So being paid cannot be an adequate criterion from separating work from other forms of human activity.

Another suggestion is that work is any activity undertaken to meet human (or mouse) needs. The field mice are working when they gather the various different types of grain that will be stored away to eat during the winter. The activity of "gathering" aims at satisfying their need for food at a time when it is no longer easily available to them.

The reason gathering counts as work is not just that it fulfills a need, but also that the mice engage in it *because* it does so and not because of, say, its inherent satisfaction. The mice in *Frederick* don't enjoy the activity of gathering, but they realize they need to do it to survive the winter.

This characterization might be thought to parallel the distinction between work and play. On this view, play, in a broad sense, is any activity undertaken for its inherent satisfaction, whereas work is undertaken for its beneficial results.

At first glance, this distinction seems quite useful. Maybe you have had a job that you didn't really enjoy but you stuck with it because you needed the money. After work, though, you probably were really dying to engage in an activity that was a form of play, be it jogging, playing ultimate Frisbee, or strumming your guitar. That activity might have even been more physically strenuous than your work, especially if you had a clerical job. But that activity wasn't work because you engaged in it for the pleasure you got from doing it.

Whenever you make a distinction, there are going to be problems handling borderline cases. These do not necessarily show that the distinction is invalid. Maybe you are a member of a book group and they have decided to read Henry James's *Portrait of a Lady*. You are part of the group because you enjoy discussing books with the group's other members. But you find James's novel deadly dull. Nonetheless, you continue reading it. But you don't do so because you find *that* activity enjoyable, but because you feel an obligation to do so. Does that make reading the book work or play?

There are also activities that start out as work that can turn into play. Maybe you play a musical instrument. You might have begun because your parents made you. If that's the case, practicing endless scales made playing that instrument work. But after a while, you may have joined a group of other musicians in performing and you found that delightful. Even though your parents no longer forced you to play your instrument, you now did so because you enjoyed it. An activity that was work has been transformed into play.

My point here is that, even if we agree that the work–play distinction is an important one, not every activity will fit nicely into one category or the other. There are many activities, such as reading *Portrait of a Lady* for the hypothetical book group, that share some features of work and some of play.

There is another feature of our evolving understanding of work that we need to think about. We have been using a definition of work as an activity undertaken to satisfy a (human) need. But human needs come in all shapes and sizes, so to speak. There are certainly some needs that everyone has simply by virtue of being human. Having enough food to survive, sufficient clothing to withstand the elements, and a shelter that keeps one safe are generally thought of as *basic human needs*. These are the types of things that the mice in *Frederick* need to get through the winter.

At the other end of the spectrum, there are things that you enjoy but don't really need. Do you like listening to classical music? Should having the ability to do so count as a human need? Most of us will agree that, at a minimum, humans don't have a basic need to listen to that specific genre of music, since probably the majority of humankind has not ever heard it. But what about having truly engaging spare-time activities? Is that a human need?

In thinking about these questions, remember how Frederick helps his fellow mice make it through the winter. He recites poetry to them. Is having access to poetry a basic human need that the story is allegorizing?

Maybe we should think of our waking hours as divided into work time and leisure time, so that the activities we pursue during our leisure time won't count as work. But there is also a problem with this suggestion. Consider eating. It certainly is an activity that I engage in to meet a basic need. But, at least some of the time, I enjoy it, especially if the food is well prepared. Does this count as work? Play? Neither?

A somewhat different way to decide which human activities should count as work begins by differentiating those things that are needed for human survival and those things that are enjoyable but not necessary in order to survive. So having an adequate amount of food to survive might be a necessity for a human being, but having your meals prepared by a gourmet chef would not. If we move to the perspective of society as a whole, we can say that, in order for a society to survive, it has to produce a certain amount of physical goods, things like food and shelter. Let's call those *socially necessary goods*.

From here, it's a short step to defining *work*: It is an activity engaged in to produce those socially necessary goods. If a hypothetical society only needs ten pounds of potatoes in order to survive, then the labor that is done to produce those potatoes counts as work. All other activities are not work.

This is a very interesting approach since, among other things, it means that the same activity – growing potatoes in my example – can count as work and also not count as work, but, say, as a leisure-time activity. So if you decided to grow ten pounds of potatoes not as part of what was socially necessary for the society to survive but because you wanted to make an extra-special potato soufflé for your spouse's birthday, that labor would not count as work, while the local farmer's growing of potatoes would.

We're now ready to return to Frederick. The question – one that the mice themselves raise – is whether Frederick is doing work when he gathers the sun, colors, and words. Since the book has used the word "gather" as its way of conceptualizing work, it might seem that Frederick is working, for he, too, is also gathering things, just not the things that all the other mice do. On the other hand, it certainly appears that he is not working. He just sits around staring into space. Before he actually recites his poems and helps the mice visualize the sun and different colors, there is no evidence that he is working. At one point, he even seems to be asleep. How can lying around and even sleeping count as working?

With the framework we have developed, we can see how to assess whether or not Frederick is working. The issue is not whether he is toiling at a difficult physical task, for clearly he is not. The right question to ask is whether Frederick is performing a task that needs to be performed in order for the mice to survive.

Frederick gives a definite answer to this question. Frederick does work, for his gathering activities are necessary for the mice to survive the winter. With their supplies running out, the mice become depressed and only Frederick's efforts allow them to stay alive until the spring. So, the book's point of view is that Frederick does work.

Now, you could argue that, had Frederick gathered some grain, there would have been more for the mice to eat and it would not have been necessary for him to recite poetry to keep them from dying of the cold and lack of food. But this response misses the point. What if Frederick's gathering of grain would not have resulted in enough food, but had kept him from writing the poem he later recites? Then, the mice would have died despite the fact that Frederick had refrained from his abstruse gatherings.

Alternatively, we can say that even though Frederick is doing *intellectual*, rather than *physical* work, both types of work are necessary for the continued existence of anything but the most simple society. Through this tale of a mouse family, Leo Lionni is making an important claim about the significance of intellectuals and artists for human life and the existence of society.

Lionni's point is that, even though intellectuals – a term I take to include artists, writers, poets, teachers, and musicians – are not doing physical labor, they are working nonetheless. The charge implicitly raised in regard to Frederick – that it's not fair that he is not working – is thus off base. Frederick is as fully engaged in his work as his fellow mice are in theirs; it's just work of a different kind.

This is a separate question from whether the remuneration people receive for their work should depend on the type of work they do. *Frederick*'s mouse society fits the famous description that **Karl Marx** gives of a communist society: "From each according to his abilities, to each according to his needs." That is, the mice share their food – and Frederick's poetry recitation – in a more or less egalitarian manner; Frederick and the other mice simply make different contributions to their society.

Our society is not, of course, structured like the mouse family, for people in our society receive differential rewards depending on the type of work they do. A neurosurgeon earns a great deal more money for operating on people's brains than does, say, a childcare worker for taking care of children. And this is true even though both tasks are arguably necessary for the continued existence of society. So, we need to ask: What justifies employing a differential rewards system for different types of work?

Exploring answers to this question would require us to consider a range of issues besides the simple question posed by *Frederick*'s mouse society: Is intellectual activity such as writing poetry a form of work? In supporting *Frederick*'s affirmative answer to this question, we have only begun to investigate the complex questions that social and political philosophers ask about work and justice. In the next chapter, we will continue to investigate issues in social and political philosophers by looking at discrimination, what it is, why it's wrong, and what should be done about it.

Discussing Work with Children

Children have differing opinions about whether Frederick was working or was just being a slacker. So discussing the story with them is a way to raise interesting issues in social and political philosophy. If you want to go farther, you might ask them why playing a sport is work for a professional athlete and fun for you and them? Is it being paid? Then what about unpaid housework? Isn't that also work even if it's not paid? Ask them to try to find a criterion for distinguishing work from other activities.

14

The Sneetches

Isn't It All Right to Discriminate in Choosing Your Friends?

Isn't it all right to discriminate in choosing your friends?

The Sneetches by Theodor Geisel (otherwise known as Dr Seuss) is a satirical story that targets illicit discrimination. A person is *discriminated against* when she or he is impacted detrimentally by actions, policies, or practices that are based upon her or his membership in a group, class, or category. In the United States and many other contemporary societies, people are discriminated against on the basis of their class, race, religion, gender, sexual orientation, national origin, or disability, among other things. Generally speaking, unwarranted discrimination is one of the primary forms of injustice from which people suffer. We will continue the discussion of social and political philosophy that we began in the last chapter by focusing on this important issue.

A Sneetch Is a Sneetch and Other Philosophical Discoveries: Finding Wisdom in Children's Literature, First Edition. Thomas E. Wartenberg. Illustrations © Joy Kinigstein.
© 2013 John Wiley & Sons, Inc. Published 2013 by John Wiley & Sons, Inc.

Discrimination

Discrimination in the morally objectionable sense occurs when a person is denied something – a job, education, a place on a bus, etc. – because he or she is a member of a social group that is deemed inferior. Discrimination is one of the most serious social injustices. Although less obvious than overt violence, discrimination harms individuals and deprives them of goods and opportunities they deserve to have.

Social and political philosophers have raised many questions about discrimination. Perhaps the most basic involves characterizing its nature precisely. There are certainly times when we think it is all right to discriminate against members of a social group, as when we deny blind people driving licenses. The task of developing a precise account of discrimination that distinguishes its morally objectionable instances from benign ones is important for both theoretical and practical reasons.

Another question raised about discrimination is whether it has to be intentional. For example, when a college turns down a Jewish applicant because admitting him would exceed their *quota* for Jews, that is a case of intentional discrimination. It is intentional because the policy has the specific goal of limiting the number of Jews at the institution. Many colleges and universities in the United States practiced such *anti-Semitic* discrimination into the 1960s.

Many social and political philosophers think that there are also many instances of *institutional* or *structural* discrimination. Their claim is that the broad patterns in the distribution of goods in society that disadvantage members of a group are also forms of discrimination. In such instances, even if no individual actor makes a discriminatory decision, the very structure of society and its institutions is discriminatory. Consider curbs. Until pretty recently, most city streets had sidewalks with curbs, on which pedestrians could walk and thus avoid being hit by cars. When they were designed, no one intended to make cities inaccessible for disabled people, but that was the result. It seems apparent that features of urban design like curbs discriminate against disabled people even though no one intended them to. This is an example of *structural* discrimination.

The Sneetches presents its parable about discrimination by depicting a society in which one group discriminates against another group because of an easily perceptible difference between them. Because the Star-Belly Sneetches have green stars on their bellies, they believe themselves superior to the poor Plain-Bellies, who have none "on thars." The Star-Bellies discriminate against the Plain-Bellies by not playing with them or inviting them to their parties. This makes the Plain-Belly Sneetches unhappy, and they mope around not having games to play or parties to attend.

The simplicity of the Sneetch society allows questions concerning discrimination to emerge with particular clarity. The basis for the Star-Belly Sneetches' discrimination against their fellows is simple. They take the presence or absence of a star to indicate superiority and inferiority, respectively. As a result, the Star-Bellies discriminate against the Plain-Bellies in the activities in which they engage: playing together and having parties.

There are two fundamental issues concerning discrimination that emerge even on such a minimal acquaintance with the book. The first is whether the presence or absence of a star on one's belly really makes one a better Sneetch for playing or partying with. Sometimes, it makes sense to discriminate. For example, you probably discriminate against some people by not choosing them to be your friends. You might prefer, for instance, not to be friends with people who do not like to talk about their feelings.

This sort of discrimination is normally perfectly justifiable. You have a criterion for friendship – being able to converse about one's feelings – and there are people who fail to meet that criterion. It makes perfectly good sense for you to choose not to be their friends. There is nothing *unfair* or *immoral* about your choosing to be friends only with people who meet your criterion.

But what if you rejected someone's overture of friendship because he was African American? Or Jewish? Or gay? Or disabled?

The standard criticism of your action in this case would be that your rejection of that person as a friend was immoral or unjust because you discriminated against him in an unjustifiable manner. This is because you treated his race, religion, sexual orientation, or disability as adequate grounds for rejecting him as a friend. But having these characteristics is irrelevant to a person's ability to be your friend. Just because he is, say, African American doesn't mean he is less capable of being a good friend to you. His belonging to that racial group is *irrelevant* to his suitability as a friend. Because you have rejected someone as a friend because of his membership in a specific social group, you have done something unjust, morally wrong.

Friendship

Many of us do not think of *friendship* as having an ethical dimension. We believe we should be free to choose whomever we want as our friends, and that whether or not we have friends is really something that is completely up to us.

Since the time of **Plato** and **Aristotle**, however, philosophers have thought that friendship was a significant topic for moral philosophy to consider. Aristotle even claimed that friends were necessary for living a fulfilling life. What reasons might he and other philosophers have had for thinking of friendship as a moral issue?

One reason Aristotle gives is that friends are important because they will resist believing slanders made against their friends. Sometimes, someone may say something negative about you that is not true. In such situations, your friends are less likely than other people to believe the slander. Their support may be crucial to you as you attempt to fight the slander.

Another reason that friends are important is that only through your conversations with your friends do you really discover who you are and how you should evaluate things that you have done. You probably have had the experience of doing something that you were not sure was right. Did you discuss your action with a friend or two? If you did, you probably discovered that friends can help you reach an accurate assessment of your own actions and your own character. Because they know you well, they are able to understand you in ways that may often be obscure even to you until you hear what your friends have to say.

This also explains why choosing friendship is taken to be a moral issue by many philosophers. Without friends whose judgment you can trust, you would not be able to see yourself clearly. Since you need that clarity of vision in order to assess your own motivations, having friends is necessary for you to act in a moral way. So, despite appearances, choosing the right friends may be an ethical matter.

Someone might reply to what I've said along the following lines: "Can't membership in a group sometimes be a legitimate reason to discriminate against someone? For example, all my close friends engage in rigorous physical activity. Because I'm so busy, I don't have time to form friendships with people who can't hike, ride a bike, or kayak with me. Although a disabled person might be perfectly nice, I discriminate against him by not choosing him as a friend. But that's justified because his disability is relevant to my choice of friends."

Tempting as it may be to accept this as an instance of legitimate group-based discrimination, I don't think we should. After all, there are many disabled people who are capable of vigorous physical activity. A blanket rejection of the disabled as potential friends just won't pass muster.

This attempted justification of a discriminatory policy also shows why most forms of discrimination in regard to choosing one's friends are morally wrong. Most of the time, if we discriminate against a person on the basis of their class, race, religion, gender, sexual orientation, disability, etc., even only in deciding whether they might qualify as our friend, we will have acted immorally, treated the person unfairly, because the decision was not made on the basis of the characteristics of the individual him- or herself.

In the United States, we don't think that discriminating immorally in choosing friends is something that should be legislated against. In this case, there is a distinction between the *morality* of an action and its *legality*. There are no laws against a person discriminating against others in her choice of friends, although you would likely think less well of her if she did. Not so with discrimination in hiring, housing, education, public services, or accommodations, among other things. That is, if a person is discriminated against in any of these areas, not only have they been treated *unfairly*, but they also can seek *legal redress* for their mistreatment. The legitimacy of this distinction is one of the subjects investigated in the *philosophy of law*, an important sub-field of social and political philosophy.

Let's take a moment to survey some of the most prevalent forms of wrongful discrimination. Discrimination against *disabled* people was widespread in the United States until the passage of the Americans with Disabilities Act in 1989. That act outlawed every form of discrimination against the disabled and resulted in many changes to the architecture of buildings and entire cities in the United States. This form of discrimination is still prevalent in many other countries.

Another prevalent form of discrimination is *racial* discrimination. In the United States, African Americans have faced serious forms of racial discrimination. This discrimination was made worse by the fact that it was enshrined in the law, going all the way back to the Constitution itself. Many racial and ethnic groups other than African Americans have also been the object of racial discrimination in the United States and other countries.

Gender discrimination is another pervasive form of discrimination. It is clear that women have been discriminated against in many ways, jobs and education being but two obvious ones. I will discuss this form of discrimination at great length in the next chapter.

Awareness of discrimination based upon *sexual orientation* has increased in recent times. Previously, people had assumed that *heterosexuality* was the normal form for human sexual relations. But now, many people think that there is a diversity of healthy sexual practices, all of which are equally valid. As a result, discrimination against homosexuals has waned, at least in many quarters.

Too many different groups have been the targets of discrimination for me to discuss each of them here. Instead, let's consider some of the strategies that social and political philosophers have adopted for criticizing discrimination. We have already considered the criticism of discrimination for being *unjust* or *morally wrong*. A different criticism is based on its *irrationality*. The idea is that discrimination is a policy that actually harms the person who adopts it.

This is the strategy that Geisel/Dr Seuss uses in *The Sneetches*. The story shows how an unscrupulous entrepreneur is able to exploit all of the Sneetches because of the presence of discrimination.

When Sylvester McMonkey McBean arrives, it appears a dream come true for the Plain-Belly Sneetches. He has a machine called the "Fix-It-Up Chappie" that can put a star on the belly of each Plain-Belly for only $3. With an added star, the Plain-Belly will pass for a Star-Belly and be able to play with them and go to their parties.

Things prove more complicated than that, though. When the Plain-Belly Sneetches appear wearing stars on their bellies, the Star-Belly Sneetches become very upset. They no longer have a way of telling who really belongs to their own, superior group. How will they be able to keep the Plain-Bellies from playing their games and going to their parties if they don't know who Star-Bellies are?

Once again, sly old McBean has a solution. For only $10 each, he will remove the stars from the bellies of the Star-Belly Sneetches. Of course, the Star-Bellies take him up on his offer and become Plain-Bellies. The former Star-Belly ones – now with their stars removed – are the toast of the town, playing games and having parties to which no one with a star can come.

Chaos ensues as the Sneetches frantically put on and take off their stars – always for a price – in their attempt to maintain or erode a system that discriminates against Sneetches just because they have or lack a star on their belly. Eventually, none of the Sneetches can tell who belongs to which group and all their money has been spent in a futile effort to reinforce or subvert the social distinction between Plain- and Star-Bellies.

McBean's unscrupulous actions bring the *irrationality* of the Sneetches' discriminatory policy to the fore.

Discriminating against Plain-Belly Sneetches is irrational because it allows the Star-Belly Sneetches to be ruthlessly taken advantage of by McBean, who is only too happy to repeatedly use his machine, so long as the price is right. The Star-Belly Sneetches would be better off if they didn't discriminate against the Plain-Bellies, for they would then have no need for the unscrupulous McBean's services.

Some would argue that there are parallels to this type of irrationality in the real world. In the 1930s, steelworkers' labor unions discriminated against African American steelworkers by not letting them join the union. The steel companies were then able to hire African American workers as "scabs" because they felt no allegiance to striking white workers. As in *The Sneetches*, racial discrimination allowed a third party to exploit the situation, to the detriment of those doing the discriminating.

But the real irrationality of discrimination in both *The Sneetches* and real life is that it is based on the false claim that members of the discriminated-against group are inferior to members of the discriminating group. This point is made at the end of the story.

As McBean then takes off, laughing at the Sneetches from whom he has profited handsomely, he prophesies that they will never learn, that they will continue to think that one group is better than the other. But that turns out not to be true, for the Sneetches come to realize that the presence or absence of a star doesn't really matter. After all, as the book puts it, "Sneetches are Sneetches." The book ends with all of the Sneetches playing with one another, paying no attention to the presence or absence of stars on their bellies.

The lesson the book imparts is that the physical differences between the two groups of Sneetches are actually insignificant. Sneetches have much more in common than they realize. As a result, it is irrational to prefer members of one group, or to give one group advantages denied the other.

In fact, once the Sneetches realize that they are all essentially the same, their lives improve. They can play with one another without worrying whether the person they are playing with belongs to their group or the other one. All the Sneetches are better off once none of them are discriminated against.

The lesson that children draw from *The Sneetches* is clear: Discriminating against people in a different social group is wrong. People have more in common than the superficial differences used to justify discriminatory policies. People are just people, we might say.

Before leaving the topic of discrimination, it is worth considering the difficulties that arise once one acknowledges the injustices that have taken place because of wrongful discrimination. Should the victims of discrimination be compensated? Should we instead adopt a "forward-looking" policy that attempts to create a society freed from the harmful effects of discrimination? Unlike in the Sneetch society, answers in real life are not easy to come by.

There has been an ongoing, highly contested debate in the United States, for example, about what to do about the brutal injustice caused by racial discrimination against African Americans. Although there is general recognition that African Americans have suffered grievously from a history of long-term legalized discrimination, there is much less agreement about what should be done, if anything, in response.

Preferential treatment, often referred to as reverse discrimination or affirmative action, is one strategy that has been proposed for ameliorating the injustice of discrimination. The idea is that, in order to correct past injustices and to help create a society with no residual traces of past discrimination, a policy should be adopted that gives some type of advantage to members of the group that was previously discriminated against. Such practices have been endorsed, for example, in regard to hiring and education, but they have been highly controversial. Many people think that discrimination is wrong, even if it aims at helping someone rather than harming them. There have been famous legal cases in which specific types of preferential treatment have been outlawed. It remains a very controversial topic in social and political philosophy and in society at large.

In the next chapter, we will consider one form of discrimination more fully, gender discrimination, and continue our investigation of issues in social and political philosophy.

Discussing Discrimination with Children

A good place to start the discussion is by asking why the Star-Belly Sneetches discriminate against the Plain-Bellies. This might get into a discussion of why people feel a need to view themselves as superior because they are members of one group rather than another. You might also consider asking the children what they think is wrong with the attitude of the Star-Bellies. And here, when talking with children, you might want to help them distinguish the immorality of discrimination from its irrationality.

15

The Paper Bag Princess

What's Wrong with "Living Happily Ever After"?

What's wrong with "living happily ever after"?

Robert Mursch's picture book, *The Paper Bag Princess*, inverts many of the gender roles traditionally found in fairy tales: It's a prince who gets abducted in this story, not a princess, though it's the princess who must come to the rescue and save him. Although these reversals are a source of the book's humor, they also underscore claims made in *feminist philosophy*, the specific branch of social and political philosophy we'll consider in this chapter.

The story begins when the beautiful princess Elizabeth is about to marry a prince named Roland. They seem the ideal couple, at least for a fairy tale: They are very wealthy, have beautiful clothes, and live in a castle. There is nothing that they seem to lack. Unfortunately, a fire-breathing dragon destroys the castle, burns all their clothes, and makes off with Roland, whom he views as a tasty morsel.

A Sneetch Is a Sneetch and Other Philosophical Discoveries: Finding Wisdom in Children's Literature, First Edition. Thomas E. Wartenberg. Illustrations © Joy Kinigstein.
© 2013 John Wiley & Sons, Inc. Published 2013 by John Wiley & Sons, Inc.

Even at this early stage, we can see that the book dramatizes concerns raised in feminist philosophy. Normally, in a fairy tale – and *The Paper Bag Princess* is a fairy tale despite its role reversals – it's the female protagonist who is weak and vulnerable, and therefore taken captive by a villain precisely so that the male protagonist can demonstrate his strength, ingenuity, and bravery in rescuing her. But this story *deconstructs* such assumptions by means of a role-reversal, for its prince is the vulnerable victim and its princess his savior. Deconstruction, as you will recall from chapter 11, asserts that Western thought was dominated by many illicit dichotomies. *The Paper Bag Princess*'s inversion of traditional gender roles illustrates one strategy for illuminating and correcting such problematic forms of thought.

Through this deconstructive strategy, *The Paper Bag Princess* highlights an issue of central importance to feminist philosophy: that social roles – and, hence, also the depiction of them in popular media including fairy tales – are *gender-biased*. In a society, people have many different roles. Some have to do with their jobs, such as being teachers, administrators, lawyers, doctors, politicians, factory workers, police officers, etc. But people also are parents, husbands and wives, children, amateur athletes, etc.

Feminists believe that social roles are gender-biased, that they are not distributed equally among women and men. For example, the better-paid and more prestigious jobs have generally been biased in favor of men, with less well paid and less prestigious ones having a greater proportion of women. This is a concern to feminist philosophers because they are determined to overcome gender bias in all fields of human endeavor.

Years ago, the following riddle was quite popular:

A father and son have a car accident and are both badly hurt. They are both taken to separate hospitals. When the boy is taken in for an operation, the surgeon says, "I cannot do the surgery because this is my son." How is this possible?

The answer is that the surgeon is the boy's mother. Many people nowadays don't find this riddle very puzzling because it's no longer unusual for women to be doctors. But that wasn't the case not so long ago, as the popularity of this riddle attests. This riddle would be puzzling only in a society in which being a doctor – a very prestigious and well-paying job – was more or less the province of men.

Feminist Philosophy

Feminist philosophy joins traditional philosophical concerns with the political project of overcoming sexism and gender bias within philosophy itself as well as in the wider world. As such, feminist philosophy is intimately related to feminist scholarship in such disciplines as economics, political science, sociology, and literary studies, for these areas share the political perspective of feminist philosophers as well as their concerns about the presence of sexism in our thinking itself.

Feminists have made contributions to every area of philosophy, not just social and political philosophy. Take the theory of knowledge. To some, this abstract field seems immune from gender concerns. Feminist philosophers have countered by raising questions, for example, about the tradition's dismissal of "feminine" ways of knowing, which leads to women being treated as epistemically inferior to men and thus relegated to marginal positions in the theory of knowledge.

One of the more surprising contributions of feminist philosophers has been the recovery of women philosophers from previous centuries. For many years, the mostly male discipline of philosophy conceived of its own history as produced nearly exclusively by men, but feminist philosophers have documented the contributions of many women to discussions of important issues in philosophy. To cite just one example, one of the first and profoundest critics of **Descartes**'s philosophy was the noblewoman, **Princess Elisabeth of Bohemia**, to whom Descartes dedicated two of his works. Even in the twentieth century, women philosophers were not taken as seriously as men.

As a result of the efforts of feminist scholars, the record has begun to be set straight. Important women philosophers like **Simone de Beauvoir** have been accorded the status they deserve. Although feminist philosophers believe that much more work needs to be done to rectify the sexist nature of the Western philosophical tradition, their multi-pronged attack has resulted in a new awareness of gender issues in philosophy and its history.

The fact that this riddle has lost its mystery is testimony to the effect that feminism has had on our society. Women now occupy prestigious positions with much greater frequency than in the past. And in increasing numbers, men now choose employment in less economically rewarding fields such as teaching and nursing, formerly the nearly exclusive domains of women.

But gaining access to jobs that were nearly exclusively populated by men is not the only concern of feminists. For many years, their battle cry was, "59¢ to every man's dollar," because a woman was paid on average 59¢ for doing the same job that a man did for $1. Feminists demanded equal pay for equal work and, to a certain extent, they succeeded in getting that for which they wished. The differential between a woman's pay and a man's pay is now 78¢ to $1, according to the National Organization of Women (www.now.org/issues/economic/factsheet.html, last accessed November 25, 2012). Still not equal but at least somewhat closer to parity.

The economy is not, however, the only arena in which feminists have been active. Because they want to alter gender oppression wherever it exists, they have also been concerned with how popular culture – films, music, books, etc. – perpetuate gender bias in social roles.

Fairy tales exhibit gender bias, as do virtually all arenas of popular culture. The stereotypical roles of "damsel in distress" and "knight in shining armor" are paradigmatic examples of this. Think of all the dichotomies that this distinction exemplifies: woman–man, weak–strong, passive–active . . . I'm sure you can think of even more. So it's not surprising to find a picture book that attempts to counter the prevalence of such sexist assumptions.

We left Roland as he was abducted by a fire-breathing dragon, who was intent on having him for a meal. Elizabeth decides that she has to save Roland. Because all her clothes were burned by the dragon, the only thing she can find to wear is an old paper bag which she puts on, giving the book its title, and sets off to save her beloved.

In its very presentation of the "crisis" that will animate its narrative – saving Roland – *The Paper Bag Princess* undercuts assumptions about the appropriate social roles for men and women. Roland is a highly unusual "damsel in distress," while Elizabeth seems an unlikely "knight in shining armor." Because we are aware of the inversion of traditional gender roles in the book, our curiosity is piqued: We want to see how things will play out. In particular, we wonder how Elizabeth will be able to rescue Roland. After all, a paper bag is hardly a suit of armor. The odds seem stacked against her.

When Elizabeth encounters the dragon, he ignores her. He is full after eating the entire castle and ready for his afternoon nap. But Elizabeth needs to rescue Roland. How can she do that with such a reluctant opponent?

In its choice of Elizabeth's "weapon," *The Paper Bag Princess* continues its deconstruction of the fairy-tale narrative. Instead of force, Elizabeth uses a tactic that women have traditionally been depicted as employing to gain power over men: flattery.

Elizabeth asks the dragon if he is really the "baddest" dragon in the world and, receiving an affirmative reply, asks him if he can really burn whole forests. To show off, the dragon burns up so many forests that he has no flame left with which to burn her.

Next, continuing her strategic use of feminine wiles, Elizabeth asks the dragon if he is the fastest dragon alive. To show her that he is, the dragon runs so far and so fast that he collapses in a heap, dead to the world. The dragon's near-catatonic state allows Elizabeth to enter the castle to free her beloved Prince Roland.

One of the ways in which the Western tradition of philosophy has exhibited its gender bias is by its denigration of women's character traits. Consider how virtue ethics, for example, enumerates the sorts of character traits necessary to lead a fulfilling life. Among **Aristotle**'s list of virtues, we find magnanimity and truthfulness, with pettiness and mock modesty listed as deficiencies or vices. It is not too much of a stretch to see that Aristotle's list of virtues characterize the ideal *man*, while the negative traits align with his conception of a nagging wife.

Or take his claim that *friendliness* is a virtue, a character trait that is beneficial to people. Associated with this trait is the deficiency of being a *flatterer*. A "flatterer" is someone who praises another more than is appropriate in order to attain power or influence over them. From a traditional Aristotelian point of view, Elizabeth's use of flattery is a moral failing.

The Paper Bag Princess deconstructs the "friendliness-flatterer" dichotomy, for Elizabeth's use of flattery is an indication of her cunning and intelligence, not a deficiency in her character. In so doing, it adopts a line of thought first developed by **Simone de Beauvoir** in her epic study of the situation of women, *The Second Sex*. De Beauvoir argues that the character traits typically associated with women – being a nag, using flattery, being seductive – are not the result of women being inherently inferior to men or having moral deficiencies in their character. Rather, these traits are the result of the inferior position to which women are consigned in a male-dominated society. Because they have been relegated to social positions with little power, women have been forced to develop strategies for gaining power and control over their lives. These putatively negative character traits associated with women are nothing more than the logical response of the powerless to their situation.

Elizabeth's use of flattery to defeat the dragon confirms de Beauvoir's analysis. The dragon has an inflated ego – a character trait that many feminist philosophers associate with men who erroneously assume that their powerful social positions are due to their own superiority rather than to their gender. Elizabeth's triumph over the dragon shows that flattery can be successfully employed by a less powerful person as a means of overcoming unjust domination by a more powerful opponent. The dragon's susceptibility to her flattery indicates *his* flawed character, not hers.

The Paper Bag Princess continues its deconstruction of sexist gender roles when Elizabeth enters the castle to rescue her beloved Roland. Instead of the gratitude that she expects Roland to have – she has, after all, saved him from being supper for his omnivorous captor – she is greeted with hostility and criticism: Roland is upset with Elizabeth's appearance rather than thankful that she has saved him. He tells her that she looks terrible, smells like ashes, has messy hair, and is wearing nothing but a filthy old paper bag for a dress. He orders her to come back when she is dressed more appropriately.

"Just like a man," I expect many of my female readers to be thinking. "You save their butt and they complain that you messed up your make-up!" Roland clearly shows himself to be an ingrate. Instead of showering Elizabeth with praise for the intelligence and cunning she used to outwit her more powerful adversary and save his life, Roland greets her with a series of criticisms for her failure to adhere to traditional notions of feminine beauty.

Here, too, *The Paper Bag Princess* has both exposed and undermined an aspect of gender oppression. Even though Elizabeth's exploits only succeed because she has rejected traditional social roles and expectations, Roland reacts to her failure to satisfy them rather than to what she has accomplished by means of her transgression. Elizabeth is so focused on saving Roland that she does what is necessary to accomplish that task, not worrying about what she looks like or is wearing. Roland, however, takes his rescue in stride. After all, it's only what he deserves. His knee-jerk reaction is animated by sexist notions of female beauty.

The Paper Bag Princess here endorses a controversial claim made by feminists: that traditional notions of beauty support the oppression of women. A beautiful woman, on this view, must conform not to her own norms, but to standards that men impose upon her. She must appear pleasing to men. Feminists capture this idea by talking of a "male gaze." Roland is clearly in the thrall of this idea, for he only reacts to Elizabeth's appearance, not to her accomplishment.

Is Elizabeth similarly held captive by the male gaze? Not at all. Although she notes how different she looks from him, with his neat hair and beautiful clothes, she tells him he's a bum nonetheless. After all she has done to save him, Elizabeth doesn't succumb to Roland's imperiousness.

The book concludes: "They didn't get married after all."

Once more, we find *The Paper Bag Princess* continuing its deconstruction of not only gender norms but also the form of the fairy tale. Most romantic fairy tales have a very different ending, the stereotypical, "And they lived happily ever after." Feminist philosophers and literary scholars have pointed out that these happy endings reassert harmful gender norms. Normally, the happy ending of a romantic tale involves a woman subordinating herself to a man in a traditional heterosexual couple.

Elizabeth will have none of this. Her rejection of Roland marks her as a truly feminist hero, for she won't let him treat her in a demeaning manner even though she has staked her own life on saving him. With his sexist attitudes, Roland is not a suitable partner for this feminist woman.

Elizabeth's refusal to conform to Roland's demands, then, points to a new philosophical issue: Why do people conform to oppressive social norms? This is the issue we will take up in the next chapter.

Discussing Feminist Philosophy with Children

You might start a discussion of feminist philosophy by asking the children to list all of the typical features of fairy tales. Things like the "happily-ever-after" ending and the "knight in shining armor." You then could ask them to list all of the ways in which *The Paper Bag Princess* is different. Comparing the two lists, you could ask them why they think the book makes so many changes. From there, you can hopefully steer them into a discussion of gender bias and oppression, and how traditional stories function to support it.

16

The Big Orange Splot

Is There Anything Wrong with Conformity?

Is there anything wrong with conformity?

In Daniel Manus Pinkwater's quirkily illustrated book, *The Big Orange Splot*, a strange accident leads a man to change his life. Mr Plumbean, the book's protagonist, discovers that he does not need to live his life in conformity with his neighbor's standards and expectations. This realization illustrates a theme central to *existentialism*, the school of philosophy that is the subject of this chapter: nothing is essential to human beings other than their freedom.

At the start of the book, Mr Plumbean is the picture of conformity. A bald, reddish-haired man whose extremely large handlebar mustache is the most distinctive thing about him, he lives on a street on which all the houses look identical. Each one has a green roof and a reddish-brown facade with four windows, each of which is partitioned into four equal squares. We are told that Mr. Plumbean and his neighbors on the street like the uniformity of their houses because it makes their street look orderly and neat.

A Sneetch Is a Sneetch and Other Philosophical Discoveries: Finding Wisdom in Children's Literature, First Edition. Thomas E. Wartenberg. Illustrations © Joy Kinigstein.
© 2013 John Wiley & Sons, Inc. Published 2013 by John Wiley & Sons, Inc.

Existentialism

From its inception, Western philosophy has emphasized *reason* and *rationality* as definitive of the human being. *Existentialism* dissents from this view, arguing that very important aspects of human life cannot be comprehended rationally. Life, the existentialists claim, is *absurd*.

By stressing life's absurdity, the existentialists hoped to push human beings to live what they term *authentic* lives. The existentialists were struck by the increasing conformity they saw prevalent in the lives of their contemporaries. Such conformity was, according the existentialists, a denial of the distinctiveness of human beings, a reduction of human beings to the level of things.

In place of the Western tradition's conception of reason as the essential property of human beings, existentialists posited freedom. Unlike all the other things in existence, according to the existentialists, human beings possessed the freedom to make of themselves what they would. **Jean-Paul Sartre**, the most famous existentialist, captured this point aphoristically: "Man's existence precedes his essence." (You will remember the idea of an essential property or essence from chapter 2.) The idea is that we exist and then create ourselves – our essence – through the free choices that we make in living our lives. Even being a conformist is a free choice that we make, according to Sartre and the other existentialists.

Existentialism achieved widespread notoriety after the Second World War through the activities and writings of Sartre and his fellow Parisian existentialists, **Simone de Beauvoir**, **Albert Camus**, and **Maurice Merleau-Ponty**. These four fellow travelers wanted existentialism to be more than the abstract academic discipline that philosophy had widely become. They attempted to rekindle the Ancient Greek notion of philosophy as the quest to determine the appropriate way to live. And they publicized their views in novels, plays, newspaper articles, and other highly public ways.

The existentialists' notoriety stemmed, in part, from Sartre and de Beauvoir's very public pact affirming their "essential" love and commitment to each other while rejecting marriage and maintaining the freedom to pursue other "inessential" sexual liaisons. Intended as a demonstration that it was possible to live a life fully embracing one's freedom, recent critics have given the pact a less positive interpretation.

Philosophically speaking, the opening pages of *The Big Orange Splot* depict a street dominated by social conformity. All its inhabitants live in identically painted homes for no other reason that they like how neat the identical façades make the street appear.

People whose lives are structured in accordance with social norms and expectations fail to live up to the potential that is inherent in every human being, the existentialists claim. What's interesting about this type of conformity is that, while everyone appears to live under its sway, it's not apparent exactly how this pressure to conform is created. **Martin Heidegger**, a philosopher often associated with existentialism, coined the term "the One" (*das Man* in German) to explain it. The idea is that people conform because they have the sense that that is what *one* does, how *one* behaves. This domination over individuals' ways of living their lives by a vague sense of how "one" does things is one pole in the existentialists' diagnosis of the ills of contemporary society.

The Big Orange Splot shows that there are other possibilities for living a fully human life. A very strange event starts trouble brewing. A seagull carrying a can of bright orange paint drops it on Mr Plumbean's house, making a big orange splot upon its roof, an event that gives the book its name. The narrative says that "no one knows why" the seagull was flying over Mr Plumbean's house carrying a can of paint, nor why it dropped it on his roof.

From the existentialist's point of view, the apparent randomness of this occurrence is characteristic of human life. Although we inevitably seek to find reasons why things happen to us and what their significance is, many of the crucial things that impact our lives can't be explained rationally and don't have any meaning inherent in them. They just take place with no rhyme and for no reason at all.

Since we resist accepting this conclusion, the existentialists used a special concept to characterize the randomness that human life is subject to: *the absurd*. For them, the absurdity of life means, quite specifically, that what happens to us cannot be seen as part of some rational plan. Things occur randomly and don't add up to anything. For many of the existentialists, this point is driven home by the fact of our own deaths. After all, they say, the finality of our own deaths undermines traditional attempts to view life as being rational and having a meaning.

Although this seems a depressing prospect to most people, it was liberating for the existentialists. We will see why if we pay attention to how Mr Plumbean reacts to the absurdity of a seagull dropping a can of bright orange paint on the roof of his house. At first, he does nothing at all. This gets his neighbors very upset, and they repeatedly tell him that he needs to get rid of the splot and repaint the roof of his house.

Eventually, Mr Plumbean takes their advice and repaints his house – but not just the roof. He decides to repaint his entire house. And instead of just repainting it the standard brown-red with a green roof, Mr. Plumbean leaves the orange splot on his roof and adds some additional ones. He also paints the facade of his house a variety of bright colors, adding pictures of a lion, three elephants, and a woman's head. In fact, he paints an entire jungle on the side of his house.

His neighbors react with indignation, as you can imagine, for they think that Mr Plumbean has gone crazy, a fact that they express in very colorful language. But they have not seen anything yet, for the very next night Mr Plumbean adds a colorfully painted clock tower atop the roof of his home. He also plants all sorts of tropical trees in his front yard, strings a hammock between the two palm trees he has planted, and brings an alligator to live on his front lawn.

When the neighbors approach Mr Plumbean to confront him about what he has done, they find him sitting in his hammock sipping lemonade. In response to them saying how upset they are, he simply replies that his house is him and he is his house, and that it looks like his dreams.

Clearly, something significant has happened to Mr Plumbean. Once the model neighbor, he now pays his neighbors no mind and does completely as he pleases. His only justification is that his house now resembles his dreams.

Existentialist philosophy gives us an insightful way to think about what has transpired. Before his roof received its orange splot, Mr Plumbean, like all of his neighbors on the street, lived a life of total conformity. His conformity was represented by the appearance of his house, which was completely identical to the appearance of his neighbors' houses.

The seagull's dropping of the orange paint is an absurd occurrence in Mr Plumbean's life, one that has no intrinsic meaning of any kind. It just happens, period. But Mr Plumbean thinks about this chance occurrence and realizes there is no reason why his house needs to look just like the houses of all of his neighbors. In fact, he can redesign his house in any way that he pleases and what his neighbors think is simply not relevant.

Just as the plain façade of his house represented Mr Plumbean's earlier life, his redesigned house, complete with palm trees, crocodiles, and a hammock, stands for the transformed life he now lives. Mr Plumbean has decided to live his life in accord with his dreams and deepest desires.

One of the things that the existentialists point out is that there is nothing that stops us from living our own dreams. Nothing, that is, but ourselves. It is our own timidity, our own vulnerability to the opinion of others that keeps us "in line," traps us in lives that we don't really like. Through a completely random event, Mr Plumbean was led to realize that he was caught in this very trap and that nothing really prevented him from living a very different life, from remaking his house in the shape of his dreams.

Continental and Analytic Philosophy

The existentialist tradition is part of a broader tradition of philosophical thinking known as Continental Philosophy. That term refers to a mode of philosophical reflection developed in Continental Europe. Although it's difficult to characterize an entire tradition both accurately and briefly, Continental philosophers focus on the actual experience of being human and try to draw philosophical conclusions from it. This tradition has its source is **Hegel**'s *Phenomenology of Mind*, a book that attempted to integrate all human experience into a single, systematic whole.

Analytic philosophy began in the early years of the twentieth century with the discovery that new techniques in formal logic could be applied to an analysis of language (see chapter 4). The initial project of analytic philosophy was to resolve all traditional philosophical questions by paying close attention to their linguistic formulations. Although this hope was soon shown to be chimerical, analytic philosophy has flourished as a distinctive philosophical methodology. It puts a premium on using language precisely and carefully as well as on formulating clear arguments to support philosophical theses.

Although there was a great deal of animosity between these two traditions during the twentieth century, they have become closer to each other in recent years. Many philosophers hope that a new, synthetic mode of philosophy will predominate in the twenty-first century.

The existentialists use a basic dichotomy to characterize the options they see human beings as having for structuring their lives. We can choose to live the sort of life that Mr Plumbean and his neighbors lived prior to the advent of the seagull. This is a life characterized by conformity with other people, living a life dominated by what Heidegger called "the One."

Although people experience conformity as something that they need to accept, as Mr Plumbean discovers, there is actually nothing to stop anyone from living the life they've always dreamed of. You can have an alligator in your garden and sip lemonade on your hammock if that's what you want. The One really has no power other than that which you give to it.

The alternative way of living your life is what the existentialists call "authenticity." To live authentically, you have to reject the suggestions that come to you from the opinion of others and pay attention only to desires that you yourself have. In Mr Plumbean's case, the clock tower and tropical garden were clearly desires hidden deep within him that only emerged once the orange splot allowed him to realize that he didn't need to conform to his neighbors' standards.

Now you may be thinking that the One – Heidegger's graphic way of depicting the pull of conformity – is not nearly as faceless as the existentialists present it. Aren't Mr Plumbean's neighbors the actual "Ones" who want him to conform? Won't they try to get him to do that?

To answer this question, let's see what happens in *The Big Orange Splot*. Not content to leave things where they are, the neighbors try to get Mr Plumbean to repaint his house just like it was before, in conformity with the façades of all the other houses. They get his next-door neighbor to pay him a visit to convey their message.

What happens next is surprising. Mr Plumbean and his neighbor sip lemonade and talk all night. As a result, Mr Plumbean's neighbor transforms his house into a large ship. The other neighbors are aghast but hear the same reply to their outrage, only this time it comes from Mr Plumbean's neighbor: His house is him and he is his house, and that it looks like his dreams.

One by one, each of Mr Plumbean's neighbors visits him and each time the result is the same: After their talk, the neighbor transforms his house into an image of his dreams. So in addition to a jungle and a ship, the street becomes home to a hot air balloon, the Taj Mahal, a castle, and a Greek temple. And whenever strangers come and criticize the street for being messy, all the residents reply that their houses are them and they are their houses, and their houses look like their dreams.

The way in which each of Mr Plumbean's neighbors arrives at the same decision as he – that they will paint their house to resemble their dreams – indicates that there really is no force that the One exerts upon each of us other than that generated by our own acquiescence to its demands. Each of his neighbors in turn gives up his attempt to get Mr Plumbean to conform and chooses instead to realize his own private dreams through transforming his house.

Philosophers in other traditions have shared the existentialists' central message about the possibility of living our lives according to our own desires rather than standards that we accept because we think they are what others demand of us. **Henry David Thoreau**, to name just one, went so far as to move from his comfortable home in Concord, Massachusetts, to a rustic wooden cabin that he built on the shores of a nearby pond whose name has now become a watchword of sorts: Walden. His message to his friends and neighbors? "Simplify, simplify." He saw them as living lives of "quiet desperation" that could be ameliorated if only they would shed their acquisitiveness.

One of the distinctive features of existentialism as a philosophy of life is how it grounds its brief for social non-conformity in a distinctive metaphysical view of human beings. Human beings, the existentialists believe, are different from all the other things that exist. All non-human things – from rocks to mountain lions – have a predetermined nature. Think about a builder. In order to build a house, he has to have a plan for the house prior to actually building it. If he didn't have that plan either in mind or actually written down, he wouldn't know what to place where. The result would be a complete disaster. The plan for the house – its essence – precedes its actual existence.

Existentialists believe that, with the exception of human beings, all things that exist are like that. They have an essence that completely determines the nature of their existence. A dog, for example, has a nature that determines what it will look like and how it will act. Dogs' essence precedes their existence as real flesh-and-blood dogs, for how they act is completely determined by their biological natures.

What about human beings? Here things get interesting. Of course, as human beings there is a sense in which we have a nature just like dogs do.

But the existentialists think that, nonetheless, there is an important difference between humans and other things. There is nothing that determines any of the crucial features of our lives, those things that we value. When we are born, for example, we are not inherently destined to be a lawyer or a steelworker, a coward or a hero. What we become is not fixed by some preexisting essence inside of us, but is something that we bring about by our own free actions. Our own decisions make us the persons that we are.

This conception of the unique nature of human life offers us all sorts of possibilities. We have the freedom to make ourselves what we want to be. I'm sure that many of you spent a lot of time thinking about what you want out of life. And you probably made a decision at some point about how to get it. In making that decision and then living so as to actualize it, you were taking advantage of the freedom that we all have as human beings to construct our lives in accordance with our own standards.

Of course we sometimes don't fully realize this idea of a self-determined, *authentic* life. At some point in your life, you may have realized that something you were doing was not something you genuinely wanted to do, but something you were doing because someone else – a parent or loved one, perhaps – wanted you to do. If you had such a realization, you may have seen that, like Mr Plumbean, you were living a life that didn't match your dreams. And you may have even decided to jettison aspects of your lives to bring it more in accord with your dreams.

When I talked about moral luck in chapter 12, I brought up the case of Gauguin. Paul Gauguin was a successful businessman who abandoned his career and his family in order to devote himself to his painting. From the point of view of existentialism, we can see Gauguin as someone who had the courage to reject a life that adhered to the traditional patterns of success: a flourishing career and a loving family. He did so to pursue something he felt he had to. In his one shot at living, the approval of others was insufficient to justify his life.

Gauguin's dramatic choice reveals the distinctive nature of human beings: our ability to create our natures according to our ideas. In addition, it exemplifies the existentialists' belief that living our lives by adhering to standards that other people impose on us is a denial of our most fundamental nature as human beings. We are free creatures who have the ability to shape our lives according to our own lights. Not to take advantage of that fact is to betray our most distinctive and significant characteristic.

From this point of view, *The Big Orange Splot* tells us a very positive and encouraging story about how people are able to realize their nature as free and creative human beings. Although all the inhabitants of Mr Plumbean's street had accepted a conformist standard for painting their houses prior to the advent of that mysterious seagull, once they see that they can use their houses as a public expression of their deepest desires, they all choose to paint their houses in ways that realize their own unique conception of life.

The word that philosophers use to characterize what Mr Plumbean and his neighbors have become is *individuals*. In abstract metaphysical terms, an individual is a single existing thing. The specific watch that I am wearing on my wrist is an individual in this sense, even though it is also a watch and thus a member of a class of similar things, watches. So you might think that the notion that Mr Plumbean and his neighbors became individuals as a result of repainting their houses is vacuous, since they were individual human beings all along.

But the sense of "individual" that is at issue in regard to Mr Plumbean and his neighbors – and in existentialism – is a different one. To be an individual in this sense is to be someone whose life reflects his own, to use the language of the book, *dream*. That is, rather than doing what is expected of you simply because it is expected of you, individuals reach deep inside of themselves to figure out what they really want. So an individual in this sense is someone who rejects conformity.

Why is it important to be an individual? This is a deep and difficult question. *The Big Orange Splot* suggests that each of us has a dream that we keep hidden away because of the pressure to conform. When we break away and allow ourselves to express our dreams, to live them, not only do we become individuals, and thus different from everyone else, but we also find the deep satisfactions of having created our own lives for ourselves – a fact the book metaphorically expresses through the fantastic houses that come to populate Mr Plumbean's street.

So charming and funny as *The Big Orange Splot* is, it presents an important claim that the existentialists and other philosophers have embraced: That the life of conformity is one that people ought to avoid, despite its attractiveness. Instead of living a life just like everyone else and fulfilling expectations that others have for us, our lives should resemble the transformed façades of all the homes on Mr. Plumbean's street: reflections of our own, individual dreams.

Discussing Existentialism with Children

A good question to pose to begin your discussion is why Mr Plumbean repainted his house and turned his garden into a tropical jungle. You might follow this up by asking why his neighbors initially disapproved but then followed his example. A final question might be if they have any dreams that they are not living and, if they do, why not.

Taking Picture

Books Seriously

You are just about finished with your tour of philosophy. It consisted of a series of encounters with children's picture books. You've seen that those books raise philosophical questions from virtually all the central fields of philosophy: metaphysics, theory of knowledge, ethics, social and political philosophy, aesthetics, even logic.

I hope that you have been as impressed as I have come to be about pictures books as philosophical texts. It has taken me a long time to fully appreciate that picture books really do require philosophical thinking to fully address the issues their narratives raise.

I began working with picture books because they are an excellent way to engage young children in philosophical discussions. Since most picture books tell stories, it's quite easy to get children interested in discussing a philosophical question that is closely tied to the narrative of a book you have read aloud with them. But when you do this, you are generally treating the books as simply a kid-friendly way to initiate a philosophical discussion.

Over the years, I have come to see that the connection between picture books and philosophy is more intimate than that. There are some picture books that require a philosophical response because they present a puzzle or conundrum that can only be resolved through a serious philosophical engagement.

"Cookies" is a good example of this. In my discussion of the story, I asked you whether you thought it made sense to say that Frog had will power at the end of the story even though he no longer had any cookies to tempt him. In order to answer this question, you had to engage in some

A Sneetch Is a Sneetch and Other Philosophical Discoveries: Finding Wisdom in Children's Literature,
First Edition. Thomas E. Wartenberg. Illustrations © Joy Kinigstein.
© 2013 John Wiley & Sons, Inc. Published 2013 by John Wiley & Sons, Inc.

careful and systematic thinking about will-power, ultimately arriving at a distinction between exercising it and possessing it.

As you have seen, not every picture book calls forth philosophy in this way. Sometimes, we need philosophy in order to analyze a disturbing message that we worry the book might have. Such was the case in my discussion of *Miss Nelson Is Missing!* The relationship between picture books and philosophy takes different forms, but it is nearly always there.

I'm inclined to think that no one who has read a picture book to their children at bedtime has pursued the sort of philosophical inquiries presented in this book, at least then and there. You're just too tired and focused on getting your child to sleep for that. But that doesn't mean that you can't pick up the thread the next morning or sometime during the day, and ask your child a question about the book you have read. Like, "Remember that story about Frog and Toad eating too many cookies? What would you have felt like if I gave the birds a bunch of cookies we had baked so that we wouldn't eat too many?"

I am suggesting that many of the best picture books are, like "Cookies," really philosophical texts in the guise of simple children's stories. As such, they deserve to be taken more seriously than they have been. They ask you to think more deeply than you probably have about genuine philosophical issues.

A large part of the joy we all take in children's books is in the delightful manner in which they call attention to philosophical issues that arise in the course of the lives of their protagonists. I hope you have seen that your enjoyment of these books can be multiplied by following the path of philosophical reflection that they mark out.

So rather than this chapter marking an ending, I hope it actually symbolizes a beginning: that of your serious encounter with picture books and philosophy.

Now that you have a sense of the range and depth of the philosophical encounters you can have by taking picture books seriously, you can pursue your interest in a couple of ways. There are many picture books in addition to the ones I have discussed here that present philosophical issues in their own unique and often quirky way. To assist in you in having more adventures in picture-book philosophy, I have included a short list of books that you are guaranteed to find mind-bending with their acute philosophical puzzles.

If you find yourself wanting to pursue your philosophical explorations without the mediation of picture books, you can check out one or more of the books I have listed in the section "Digging Deeper into Philosophy." There you will find a list of books that will keep your philosophical journey going.

Using picture books to launch yourself into a more in-depth acquaintance with philosophy is highly appropriate. For this way of approaching philosophy restores the joy and pleasure of philosophical investigation that sometimes gets lost in, say, college philosophy courses. But, as the Greek philosophers tell us, philosophy begins in wonder.

"Wonder" is an interesting word because its meanings include both perplexity and awe, two feelings that are intimately connected to philosophy. Philosophy certainly arises in being bewildered about something. In order to resolve that feeling, you have to engage in the reflective thought process characteristic of philosophy.

But awe is also an important part of philosophy. There are aspects of the world and our existence within it that simply inspire awe in us. **Kant** famously picked out two: the starry heavens above and the moral law within. Each of you may have other things that you think are at least as awe-inspiring as the sky and morality were for Kant. I would like to single out one: philosophy itself. For no matter how difficult and perplexing philosophy can be at times, it retains its capacity to delight us and inspire us with awe as we reflect on the wondrous nature of the world in which we find ourselves.

A final thought: Philosophy is not about finding the right answer to a question, although philosophers are always trying to do that. It is really about the process of thinking about perplexing issues themselves and contemplating possible solutions to them, a process that is both enjoyable and, at times, frustrating.

Most of the children with whom I have engaged in philosophical discussions have told me how much fun they have doing philosophy. I hope that reading this book has convinced you, too, that philosophy can be fun.

But philosophy is also a bug whose bite is often incurable. Once you've been bitten, you may have it for life. If that's true of you, all I can do is wish you, *Happy Thinking!*

Who's Who

Thumbnail Biographies of the Philosophers

Aristotle (384–322 BCE) was one of the most influential philosophers of all time. Relying on his experience as a biologist, he developed a systematic philosophy that provided accounts of almost all the questions of philosophy, from metaphysics to aesthetics. So great was his influence that medieval philosophers simply referred to him as The Philosopher. Aristotle was also responsible for some of the most egregious scientific errors of all time, such as the notion of spontaneous generation, the idea that things could be generated out of nothing.

J.L. Austin (1911–1960) was a British philosopher and one of the founders of the "ordinary language" approach to philosophy, along with **Ludwig Wittgenstein**. One of his central contributions was the notion of a *performative utterance*, that is, a use of language that does not just report a fact but actually does something. When, during a wedding ceremony, I say, "I do," I am not reporting the fact that I am now married, but actually creating that fact. Such insights led Austin to cast doubt on many philosophers' claims about reality.

Jeremy Bentham (1748–1832), the founder of utilitarianism, was a political reformer as well as a philosopher. He intended utilitarianism to result in social reforms that would do away with outdated policies that could not be justified on the basis of their contribution to social welfare. He was also a social reformer, whose design for a new, rational prison,

A Sneetch Is a Sneetch and Other Philosophical Discoveries: Finding Wisdom in Children's Literature, First Edition. Thomas E. Wartenberg. Illustrations © Joy Kinigstein.

the Panopticon, has been cited as paradigmatic of the increasing social control that accompanied the Enlightenment. As part of his bequest at his death, Bentham required that his body, suitably shorn of organic matter, be exhibited, which it is, to this day, at University College.

George Berkeley (1685–1753), the Bishop of Cloyne, advocated the philosophical position of idealism. Taking John Locke as his target, Berkeley argued that the only things that actually existed were what he termed "finite substances," such as you and me, and the one infinite substance, God. A skilled dialectician, Berkeley was able to present arguments that are hard to refute. Frustrated, the poet and essayist Samuel Johnson kicked a stone in order to refute Berkeley's theory that matter does not exist.

Simone de Beauvoir (1908–1986) was an important thinker in the existentialist tradition. Although for many years she was regarded more as a novelist and as Sartre's companion than as an independent thinker in her own right, feminist philosophers have argued that the originality of de Beauvoir's thought needs to be acknowledged. As well as documenting the lives of the French existentialists in a series of novels, de Beauvoir wrote one of the fundamental books of feminist philosophy, *The Second Sex*.

Albert Camus (1913–1960) was an Algerian journalist and novelist who belonged to the inner circle of existentialist thinkers in post Second World War Paris. In many ways, Camus was more of an essayist than a formal philosopher. Nonetheless, his novel *The Stranger* and his philosophical work *The Myth of Sisyphus* are central texts in the existentialist tradition. He is most famous for his claim that the only significant problem of philosophy is suicide.

Gerald Cohen (1941–2009) was a Marxist philosopher who developed an account of Marx's theory of history that would make the theory more palatable to philosophers in the Analytic tradition. He also attacked **Robert Nozick**'s defense of Libertarianism, arguing that a much more limited set of inequalities were consistent with the demands of justice. He also defended socialism from critics of all political stripes.

Arthur Danto (1924–) is one of the foremost contemporary philosophers of art as well as an important art critic. His book, *The Transfiguration of the Commonplace*, transformed the debate about whether art could be defined by arguing that no perceptual properties distinguish art works from "mere things." Working for many years as the art critic for *The Nation* magazine, Danto amassed a substantial volume of criticism that focused on contemporary art. In addition, Danto wrote books on such varied topics as the philosophy of history and the philosophy of action as well as historical figures like Nietzsche and Sartre.

Jacques Derrida (1930–2004) was a Jewish, French philosopher who founded the approach to philosophy known as "deconstruction." A sensitive and thoughtful reader of previous philosophical works, Derrida claimed that Western philosophy was founded on a set of "binary oppositions" in which one of a pair of terms is "privileged" over the other. This provided him and his followers with a powerful tool for uncovering what they claim are failures by Western philosophers to justify their own claims. He is the subject of a film that bears his last name.

René Descartes (1596–1650) began a revolution in philosophical thought by putting the human being first and asking what we can know for certain. His goal was to establish a firm foundation for the sciences, but what he succeeded in doing was to transform the way in which philosophy was done. He is therefore known as the father of modern Western philosophy. He also is the first of the three classical rationalist philosophers, with **Baruch Spinoza** and **Gottfried Wilhelm Leibniz** being the others. He is most famous for his saying, *Cogito ergo sum* (I think, therefore I am), which proved, he thought, that his own existence could be established as indubitable and certain.

Princess Elisabeth of Bohemia (1618–1680) was a noblewoman who was renowned for her wide learning. She engaged in a lengthy philosophic correspondence with **Descartes** that ended only with his death. Although he took on the role of her spiritual advisor, she was anything but subservient. She developed serious criticisms of his theories and, despite the gracious style of her epistolary interactions with him, pressed him to explain himself and his views more clearly.

Descartes took Elisabeth's criticisms seriously. He even dedicated two of his works to her, his *Principles of Philosophy* and *The Passions of the Soul*. He clearly viewed her as a worthy philosophical interlocutor.

Ralph Waldo Emerson (1803–1882), the sage of Concord, was a rather unsystematic thinker whose writings are hard to classify. He eschewed academic writing and wrote more in the style of his sometime profession as a preacher. He exhorted his fellow New Englanders to slough off their conformist lives in order to attain a more adequate way of life. Influenced by **Kant**, he saw in nature a guide to living more authentically. Along with **Henry David Thoreau**, he was one of the founders of transcendentalism, the first authentically American approach to philosophy. Among the philosophers who were influenced by him is **Friedrich Nietzsche**.

Epicurus (*c.* 341–*c.* 270 BCE) was a Greek philosopher who developed a system of hedonism, the idea that the goal of life should be the production of pleasure and the avoidance of pain. Unlike many hedonists, Epicurus thought that the surest way to maximize the pleasure one experienced was to strategically avoid feeling pain. As a result, he advocated a simple life, one that would lead to the least suffering and hence the greatest satisfaction. His doctrine was given a popular formulation by the Roman poet **Lucretius** in his poem *On the Order of Things* (*De Rerum Natura*).

Gottlob Frege (1848–1925) was a German philosopher, mathematician, and logician. His rigorous systematization of logic marked the first radical transformation of that discipline since Aristotle had invented it. Frege also developed a philosophy of language that remains influential to this day. Although his own writings were mostly ignored during his lifetime, they are now very influential, thanks to the efforts of, among others, **Bertrand Russell**.

Martin Heidegger (1889–1976) was one of the most influential philosophers of the twentieth century. He believed that previous philosophers in the Western tradition had passed over the most significant of all philosophical questions: What is the meaning of being? In attempting to answer this question, Heidegger inaugurated a "destruction" of Western metaphysics that attempted to free our way of thinking about ourselves and our world from the influence of scientific models. His writing influenced both existentialism and deconstruction, two important schools of philosophical thought. Heidegger's membership in the Nazi Party has been a controversial topic among philosophers. At issue is whether his claims about Western philosophy are colored by his regressive and anti-Semitic attitudes.

G.W.F. Hegel (1770–1831) was a German philosopher known both for the extraordinary reach of his system and the obscurity of his prose. Hegel was an "absolute idealist," someone who thought that reality exhibited a rational structure that could be captured by an acute philosopher such as himself. Among his other accomplishments, Hegel was the first philosopher to argue that history was a rational process of the creation of freedom. He thought that Napoleon represented the culmination of that process in the real world, just as Hegel's own system did in the realm of thinking.

Heraclitus (*c.* 535–*c.* 475 BCE) was an Ancient Greek philosopher about whom very little is known. He came from Ephesus, a city in Asia Minor. He is thought to have written only a single book and what we have of it are only a series of aphorisms. Perhaps his most famous states, "You cannot step into the same river twice for new waters are ever flowing."

As this aphorism makes clear, Heraclitus believed that everything was always and everywhere in a state of flux. He likened reality to a great fire that was constantly consuming some things and spitting out others.

Heraclitus was an elitist and he thought that few would understand his message. His enigmatic writing style helps validate this conclusion.

Thomas Hobbes (1588–1679) was a wide-ranging philosopher who made contributions to a number of different fields. He uses his description of the state of nature as one in which life is "solitary, poor, nasty, brutal, and short" to justify the creation of an absolute monarchy by means of a contract between human beings. Social contract theory remains the basis of most political theorizing by philosophers. Hobbes was also a materialist, someone who believes that the ultimate constituent of the universe is physical matter. His final words are reported to have been, "a great leap in the dark."

David Hume (1711–1776) was a member of the Scottish Enlightenment. Although he is known for his "skeptical" philosophy, Hume was not a thorough-going skeptic, someone who thinks that knowledge is impossible. Hume was, rather, a radical critic of the epistemology of Descartes, and sought to replace the Cartesian view of knowledge based upon certainty with one that focuses on rational probability. He was the last of the three classical empiricist philosophers, after **John Locke** and **Bishop Berkeley**. He was also an avowed atheist and sought to show that there are no rational grounds for religious belief.

Immanuel Kant (1724–1804) was a German philosopher who articulated his systematic philosophy in the great *Critiques*. Although Kant thought that humans could not have knowledge of the world as it actually was, he developed an account of human knowledge as based upon appearances. He claimed to have limited knowledge to "make room for faith," for he contended that morality and religious belief had to do with the nature of reality itself, which cannot be known empirically. His "critical philosophy" had a huge impact on subsequent generations of philosophers.

Søren Kierkegaard (1813–1855) was a Danish philosopher and theologian who claimed that faith and reason were two completely incompatible ways of living. Indeed, so radically different were they that claims made from the point of view of one could not even be understood from within the other. As a result, faith could not be attained by means of rational argumentation, as many philosophers had thought, but only by a *leap of faith*. In asserting that fundamental decisions about how to live one's life were not amenable to rational discussion, Kierkegaard inspired the existentialist school of philosophy.

Gottfried Wilhelm Leibniz (1646–1716) was a real polymath, making contributions to many different fields of knowledge. For example, in addition to his philosophical writings, he made important discoveries in mathematics, inventing, along with Isaac Newton, calculus. Leibniz was also heavily involved in political affairs, an occupation that kept him from writing a systematic account of his philosophy. He did, however, write many short accounts of his idealist metaphysics, according to which matter lacks ultimate reality. Leibniz's philosophy is also characterized as optimism for his claim that this world is the best of all possible worlds. Voltaire satirized Leibnizian optimism in *Candide*.

John Locke (1632–1704) founded the empiricist school of modern Western philosophy. In opposition to Descartes's claim that our knowledge is based on innate ideas implanted in us by God, Locke claimed that all of our knowledge is derived from experience. In providing an account of knowledge, Locke was less optimistic than Descartes, and placed severe limits on what it is possible to know. Locke was also an important social and political philosopher, whose justification of liberal democracy placed in him in sharp contrast to **Hobbes**. He was a major inspiration for the founding fathers of American democracy. In addition, Locke was a strong advocate for religious toleration.

Lucretius (?–*c.* 50 BCE) was a Roman philosopher whose great poem, *On the Nature of Things* (*De Rerum Natura*), developed a materialist philosophy derived from the ideas of the Greek philosopher, **Epicurus**. According to Lucretius, all of reality could be explained simply on the assumption that there were atoms and empty space, the void. All change, on this view, results simply from regroupings of the atoms, something that occurs as they continually fall through empty space.

One of Lucretius' most intriguing suggestions is that human free will is simply the result of the atoms taking unpredictable "swerves" in their ongoing descent. Without this, we would be completely determined by natural laws, but these swerves are what account for the presence of "free will" in humans.

Karl Marx (1818–1883) is famous as the father of Communism. What many people do not know is that he was also a philosopher. Marx's philosophical writings developed as a critique of what he saw as the reactionary writings of Hegel. Whereas Hegel thought of history as the unfolding of the rational structure of the universe, Marx saw it as a material process grounded in the economic structure of society. His account of the alienation of workers under capitalism has been very influential on later social and political philosophers.

Maurice Merleau-Ponty (1908–1961) was an important thinker in the existentialist tradition. Central to his writing is the importance of the body in our perception and thinking. This emphasis on the body corrected the tendency of the Western tradition of philosophy to treat the human being as essentially just a mind. Unlike other existentialist thinkers, Merleau-Ponty thought that philosophy needed to incorporate the results of empirical sciences like cognitive psychology. He thus anticipated important trends in contemporary philosophy.

John Stuart Mill (1806–1873) was a precocious genius, who began learning Greek at the age of 3. He was an advocate of utilitarianism, the approach to ethics founded by **Bentham**. He sought to reconcile this advocacy of the greatest good for the greatest number with an equally firm allegiance to liberty, the protection of the freedom of individuals. He was a political reformer and, together with his wife, Harriet Taylor, wrote one of the first philosophical justifications of feminism, *The Subjection of Women*.

Friedrich Nietzsche (1844–1900) was a very radical and independent thinker. Although he began his career as a professor at the University of Basel at the tender age of 24, he soon renounced his post as inimical to the independence of his thinking. Nietzsche was a radical critic of Western society, holding that it had been in a state of decline since the early days of Athenian society. At different times, he held Socrates, Jesus, and Jews responsible for that decline. He posited the possibility of a new type of society in which people would become Overmen or *Übermenschen*, individuals freed from the guilt that Nietzsche saw Judeo-Christian society as creating.

Robert Nozick (1938–2002) is most well-known for his defense of libertarianism in opposition to the theory of justice proposed by **John Rawls**. His argument was that, so long as all exchanges were engaged in freely, any inequality that resulted from them was legitimate.

Nozick made contributions to a variety of areas of philosophy besides social and political philosophy. One such contribution involved a thought experiment involving an Experience Machine. Because people would not be satisfied to merely have an experience, even if it was illusory, Nozick argued that utilitarianism's claim that pleasure was the only good was radically mistaken.

Parmenides (early fifth century BCE) was the author of a single meta-physical prose poem that delineates his philosophy. On his view, there are two *ways*, the way of being and the way of illusion. The way of true being is completely unchanging while the way of illusion treats change as real. Humans generally are limited to the inadequate way of illusion.

Despite the enigmatic character of Parmenides' thought, he influenced the subsequent development of Greek philosophy. In fact, Plato depicts him in an eponymously named dialogue as interacting with the young Socrates, whom he treats with patience and good humor.

Charles Sanders Peirce (1839–1914) founded the school of American philosophy known as pragmatism. The fundamental tenet of pragmatism is that an idea's meaning is nothing but its practical consequences. This pragmatic maxim could be used to show that a number of traditional philosophical arguments were really mock battles, for the dispute had no practical consequences. Peirce published his philosophical ideas in a variety of unusual venues, including *Popular Science Monthly*, where he published a series of essays that outlined his pragmatist approached. When William James took over the name "pragmatism" as a result of Peirce's influence, Peirce was so upset that he invented the term "pragmaticism" to describe his philosophy, hoping that its unwieldiness would keep others from borrowing it.

Plato (429–347 BCE) was a student of **Socrates**. His writings all take the form of dialogues, records of real or imaginary conversations, usually between Socrates and the young men of Athens. Although his early dialogues are generally taken to be accurate records of Socrates' interactions with his fellow Athenians, Plato's later dialogues, while retaining the form of a conversation, are actually articulations of Plato's own theory, most notably the Theory of the Forms. Plato held that the world of our everyday experience is merely an appearance of the real world of unchanging and eternal Forms. This theory has continued to exert a strong influence on philosophers to the present day. Although other philosophers have copied Plato's dialogue form, few have done it successfully.

The Pre-Socratics were a group of Greek thinkers in the fifth and sixth centuries BCE who introduced a new way of thinking into the Western tradition. They collectively are the fathers of philosophy. However, they did not distinguish clearly between philosophy and natural science, as we know them. As a result, some of their theories seem more like the initial attempts to understand the world scientifically than they do genuine philosophical works. At the same time, these philosophers began the search for truth about reality guided by rational thinking rather than mythology.

Characteristic of the pre-Socratics is Xenophanes' claim that what the poets took to be a goodness, Iris, the goddess of the rainbow, is nothing more than a cloud.

John Rawls (1921–2002) was probably the most influential social and political philosopher of the twentieth century. In his book, *A Theory of Justice*, he defended the traditional Liberal agenda of equality of political participation and substantial limits to inequalities introduced by the workings of the market place. Using a thought experiment involving a Veil of Ignorance, in which participants deliberating about the appropriate principles to govern their society in ignorance of their actual position in the social, political, and economic hierarchy, Rawls revitalized the contractarian tradition of Western political thought.

Rawls continued to revise and defend his theory until his death. Increasingly, he saw himself as working within a Kantian framework.

Bertrand Russell (1872–1970) was one of the best-known philosophers of the twentieth century. Although Russell's greatest contributions to philosophy came in the fields of logic and the philosophy of language, he wrote widely on many different topics in philosophy and society, more generally. He was awarded the Nobel Prize for Literature in recognition of his broad impact on humanistic thinking. Russell's most influential work in philosophy applied recent discoveries in logic to issues in the philosophy of language and mathematics. He thought that our ordinary ways of speaking concealed a hidden logical structure that, once revealed, allowed for the solution of most philosophical problems. This idea was one of the key ones in the development of that approach to philosophy known as analytic philosophy.

Jean-Paul Sartre (1905–1980) is the central figure in French existentialism. His writings run the gamut from formal philosophical texts to plays, novels, and journalistic essays. In each of these areas, Sartre excelled. His novel *Nausea* presented the lived context within which philosophical ideas occur to human beings. His major philosophical work, *Being and Nothingness*, includes justly famous analyses of human sexuality and emotions such as shame, showing how they are part of what it is to be human. His play, *No Exit*, is still produced and shows the validity of the famous claim, "Hell is other people." Perhaps his most famous claim is that "man's existence precedes his essence," for that snappy phrase exhibits the central premise of philosophy.

Socrates (469–399 BCE) occupies a crucial place in the history of Western philosophy for both his ideas and his life. The portrait of him presented in the dialogues of his student **Plato** shows him to be relentlessly engaged in the search for truth. His interrogations of his interlocuters have been a model for many philosophers, who take philosophy to be best expounded through rigorous discussion. His tragic death also makes him a model of philosophical commitment. Accused of impiety and corrupting the youths of Athens, Socrates chose to die by drinking hemlock rather than to give up his dogged pursuit of the truth.

Baruch Spinoza (1632–1677) is probably the most famous Jewish philosopher of all time. Identifying him in this way is ironic, since he was excommunicated by the Jewish community of Amsterdam in 1656. The reason was likely that his view of God unsettled his contemporaries, for Spinoza claimed that God and Nature were identical, being but different names for the one existing substance. Spinoza's philosophy is at once radical in its rejection of an anthropomorphic perspective and inspiring in its presentation of human existence. A thorough-going determinist, Spinoza also made room for the possibility of human freedom and, indeed, of blessedness.

St Anselm of Canterbury (*c.* 1033–1109) attempted to provide logical proofs of the existence of God. Whereas many previous Christian philosophers had accepted faith as the grounds for religious belief, Anselm wanted to provide a rational grounds for faith itself. His most noted argument for God's existence was the ontological argument, which sought to deduce God's existence from merely his concept as the greatest of all possible beings. This proof has fascinated philosophers ever since. It has had both its adherents – **Descartes** and **Leibniz**, to name two – as well as its critics – **Hume** and **Kant**, for example. Whether it is a valid argument remains an unsettled question to this day.

St Augustine (354–430) was a neo-Platonist Christian philosopher. He saw his mission as showing that the Platonic philosophy could be reconciled with Church doctrine. His *Confessions* are a fascinating document of a man's transformation by religious faith. Looking back at his earlier life, Augustine shows how he changed from a sinner to someone with profound religious convictions. The book is also studded with many interesting philosophical discussions such as that on the nature of time. Two of his contributions to philosophy and theology were the concepts of original sin and just war.

Henry David Thoreau (1817–1862) is most well-known for his attempt to lead a life not governed by the search for wealth and comfort. He documented his experiment in *Walden*, a book that records his years living by the pond of the same name in a simple cabin that he had built. He hoped to influence his neighbors, most of whose lives he characterized as lived in "quiet desperation." A life of voluntary poverty, he thought, was preferable to the slavery he saw most people as choosing. He was also a political activist, choosing to go to jail to protest the Fugitive Slave Law. When **Emerson** came to visit Thoreau, he asked Thoreau, "Henry David, what are you doing in there?" To which Thoreau quipped, "What are you doing out there, Ralph Waldo?"

William of Ockham (*c.* 1287–1347) was an English Franciscan monk and philosopher. He is best known for his ontological parsimony. This is most famously recorded in his famous "Razor," which holds that one should not needlessly multiply entities. If you can get along without positing the existence of anything, then you should, according to this maxim. Ockham was also a nominalist, someone who thought that only individuals were real, not classes or abstract entities. This view has had many proponents, all of whom trace their lineage back to William.

Ludwig Wittgenstein (1889–1951), one of the most important philosophers of the twentieth century, was so mesmerizing that he attracted many disciples. His early philosophy was similar to that of **Russell**, for he believed that logic provided a means of articulating a perspicuous language that would avoid the obscurities of natural languages. Later, he became his own most powerful critic, arguing that philosophical problems arose when language "went on holiday," i.e., vacation. He believed that philosophers had taken too individualistic an approach to understanding language. He, along with **Austin**, founded the ordinary language approach to philosophy in which philosophical problems were not to be solved but dis-solved. One of his characteristically witty sayings was that philosophy was the attempt "to let the fly out of the fly-bottle." Wittgenstein also likened philosophy to a disease and he saw his writings as a way to cure people of it.

What's What

Key Philosophical Terms

accident   A property possessed by a **substance** that it need not have. Hair color is an accidental property of human being, since it can be changed without altering a person's nature.

***ad hoc* assumption**   An assumption whose only basis is to solve a problem. It is *ad hoc* because it is devised only for that purpose and has no independent evidence to support it.

analytic philosophy   A style of philosophical investigation developed in Britain during the early years of the twentieth century that has become practiced worldwide. It puts a premium on exactitude of meaning and clarity of expression. Generally, it also emphasizes precise argumentation to establish its conclusions.

appearances   Contrasted with reality in metaphysics. Appearances are things that do not possess full-bloodied reality. Because a straight stick does not actually bend when partially submerged in a glass of water, the bent stick is an appearance.

Akrasia   *see* **weakness of the will**

atheist   Someone who does not believe in God.

Cartesian   The ideas and theories of **René Descartes**.

Continental philosophy   The dominant form of philosophizing in Continental Europe during the twentieth century. Continental philosophy focuses upon the everyday experience of human being, seeking to

A Sneetch Is a Sneetch and Other Philosophical Discoveries: Finding Wisdom in Children's Literature, First Edition. Thomas E. Wartenberg. Illustrations © Joy Kinigstein.
© 2013 John Wiley & Sons, Inc. Published 2013 by John Wiley & Sons, Inc.

draw out its presuppositions and implications. **Existentialism** and **phenomenology** are two related forms of Continental philosophy.

contingent   The idea that something is not necessary, might not have occurred. Both events and things can be called contingent, meaning that the event did not have to happen and that the thing did not have to exist.

counterexample   A technique for showing the inadequacy of a philosophical claim. An albino leopard is a counterexample to the claim that all leopards have spots, albeit an empirical one. Philosophical counterexamples are more abstract and there is often debate as to whether they are really counterexamples at all.

descriptive use of language   The use of language to state facts about something. "The sky is blue" is a descriptive statement because it attributes a specific color to an object. *See also* **evaluative use of language**.

discrimination   The wrongful treatment of an individual on the basis of their membership in a particular social group such as class, race, gender, sexuality, national origin, or disability.

dualism   A metaphysical theory about the nature of reality, attributing reality to two different **substances**, mind and matter. It is also a theory about the human being, who is also taken to be composed of both mind and matter.

empirical   Refers to questions or issues that can be settled through experience. Statements that are empirical are factual. "It is sunny today," is an empirical statement because looking out the window and seeing whether it is, in fact, sunny, determines whether it is true.

essence   As opposed to **accident**. A **substance**'s essence is that which the substance must have in order to be the thing that it is. Geometrical figures are clear example of things that have essences. A triangle would not be a triangle if it were not a three-sided, plane figure.

evaluative use of language   Makes an evaluation or value judgment about something. "That painting is beautiful" is an evaluative use of language because we take beauty to be a positive attribute of a thing. *See also* **descriptive use of language**.

existentialism   One of the main forms of Continental philosophy. See chapter 16 for a fuller discussion.

idealism   Refers to the metaphysical thesis that only minds and mind-dependent things like thoughts are real. All other apparently real things – like physical things – are reduced to being the contents of minds.

logical positivism   A view about the meaningfulness of language. Logical positivism holds that a statement is meaningful only if it has clear empirical consequences. Many statements of traditional metaphysics were thereby claimed to be meaningless.

materialism   The metaphysical theory that only physical things – matter – are real.

ontology   A branch of metaphysics concerned specifically with the question of what things exist.

performative   A term in the philosophy of language that refers to language's ability to *do* things. Uttering the sentence, "I promise," actually makes a promise, does something. It is a paradigmatic performative utterance.

phenomenology   One of the central types of Continental philosophy. It pays close attention to human experience, attempting to articulate its basic character by means of a careful exposition of its nature.

reflective thinking   The type of thinking characteristic of philosophy. It takes as its object activities and practices that we normally engage it. It questions their rationality.

representation   Used to refer to things like pictures and thoughts. They are representations because their contents refer to other things.

speciesism   An illicit privileging of human beings over other species of natural entities.

statement   What you say by uttering a sentence. Although statements usually say what the sentence means, this is not always true. Sarcasm is one example of using a sentence to make a statement with a different meaning than that of the sentence.

substance   Used by metaphysicians to refer to those things that are able to endure throughout change. Philosophers have debated about what sorts of things can count as substances and, indeed, if there are any.

tautology   An identity statement. The famous statement "a rose is a rose is a rose" is, from a logical point of view, merely a series of tautologies. Normally, tautologies appear to be making a statement but can be shown to only be concealed identity statements. This limerick consists of a series of tautologies:

> There once was a fellow from Perth
> Who was born on the day of his birth.
> He got married, they say
> On his wife's wedding day
> And he died when he quitted the earth.
> (Cited in *Wikipedia*)

theist Someone who believes in God's existence. Theists differ on whether God's existence is a matter of faith or can be proven by rational arguments.

thought experiment An experiment carried on in one's head in order to establish a philosophical claim. There is a fuller discussion in chapter 3.

weakness of the will Doing something that you think you shouldn't because it's so attractive to do. Also called *Akrasia*.

Next Steps

Additional Philosophical Picture Books

Here is a list of some popular picture books along with a brief characterization of the philosophical issues that they raise.

Alexander and the Terrible, Horrible, No Good Very Bad Day, by Judith Viorst (New York: Atheneum Books, 1987), is an amusing story about a young boy who has a truly awful day. His angry response provides an opportunity to discuss emotions with children: what they are, why we have them, how one can manage them, etc.

The Big Box, by Toni Morrison (Bel Air, CA: Jump at the Sun, 1999), poses questions about freedom and its importance through the story of three children who have theirs limited when they are placed in the box as punishment. In addition, the question of what people need to be happy is aptly posed: Why might material things not be enough? And if they aren't, what else do we need to be happy?

The Cat in the Hat, by Theodore Geisel (Dr Seuss) (New York: Random House, 1957), portrays a series of antics that the Cat engages in when the narrator's mother leaves him and his sister alone. It raises interesting questions about the difference between reality and imagination in a very amusing manner.

"Dragons and Giants," another story from Arnold Lobel's classic *Frog and Toad Together* (New York, Harper Collins, 1971), has Frog and Toad climb a mountain to determine if they are really brave. It raises a host of questions about the nature of bravery and its relation to fear. All of the Frog and Toad stories are studded with philosophical problems.

Iggy Peck, Architect, by Andrea Beaty (New York: Harry N. Abrams, 2007), features a young child who loves to build things but whose second-grade teacher thinks that that activity is inappropriate and forbids him from doing it. The book raises questions about the legitimacy of adults' decisions about what is appropriate – or not – for children.

Let's Make Rabbits, by Leo Lionni (New York: Pantheon Books, 1969), depicts things transforming from imaginary to real. It is an excellent story for discussing the difference between imaginary things – including pictures and drawings – and real ones. The book is suitable for very young children.

The Rainbow Fish, by Marcus Pfister (New York: NorthSouth, 1992), is the story of a selfish fish who learns the importance of sharing. At the same time, it's a story about loneliness and the importance of friends. Its delightful illustrations make this a great book for discussing these important issues with children.

The Real Thief, by William Steig (New York: Farrar, Straus and Giroux, 1973), is the story of a goose who is wrongly convicted of a crime. It raises questions about justice and the legal system. But it's also a story about guilt and redemption, all posed in its animal kingdom, so that children find it easy to discuss.

Roxaboxen, by Alice McLerran (New York: Harper Collins, 1991), tells the story of a woman's visit to the ruins of a town where she and her friends created an imaginary world together. While raising questions about the role of the imagination in the life of children, it also highlights questions about memory and how it can make things that happened long ago become real, at least in a person's mind.

"Uncle Ry and the Moon" is one of the stories told in Jon J. Muth's *Zen Shorts* (New York: Scholastic Press, 2005). While the entire book raises interesting philosophical issues, this story – about how Uncle Ry treats a thief he discovers in his house – raises questions about why we treat other people the way we do. It asks us to consider whether we really can treat each person as a human being like ourselves, and why we don't.

The Very Hungry Caterpillar, by Eric Carle (New York: Philomel, 1986), poses a question about identity, a topic in metaphysics. The caterpillar goes through a significant change on each page of this delightfully illustrated book. How can it be the same creature when it has been transformed into a beautiful butterfly? Puzzles abound, making this a great book to discuss with very young children.

Where the Wild Things Are, by Maurice Sendak (New York: Harper Collins, 1963), is the story of a young boy, Max, who gets sent to his room without dinner for misbehaving. Max travels to the world of the Wild Things, but finds himself wishing for home. It raises questions about anger, the imagination, and the importance of love.

Not satisfied? My website – www.teachingchildrenphilosophy.org – lists over 100 books together with introductions to their philosophical issues and suggested questions for initiating philosophical discussions. If you want a more explicit discussion of how to teach philosophy to young children, try my book, *Big Ideas for Little Kids: Teaching Philosophy Through Children's Literature* (Lanham, MD: Rowman and Littlefield Education, 2009).

More Next Steps

Digging Deeper into Philosophy

If you have been bitten by the philosophy bug and want to continue learning about it, here are some suggestions:

Books

A book that presents the history of philosophy in an approachable but very accurate manner is Donald Pamer's *Looking at Philosophy: The Unbearable Heaviness of Philosophy Made Lighter* (Reading, PA: William C. Brown Co., 1988).

Logicomix: An Epic Search for Truth by Christos H. Papadimitrious and Apostolos Doxiadis (London: Bloomsbury Publishing, 2009) is a graphic novel that explores the discovery of modern logic and the development of philosophy of language.

What Does It All Mean?: A Very Short Introduction to Philosophy, by Thomas Nagel (New York: Oxford University Press, 1987), is a more standard but very accessible introduction to philosophy or, at least, some of its central areas. Only read it if you want to have a more traditional introduction to philosophy.

There are now a variety of different books that collect mind-bending thought experiments in order to introduce people to philosophy. One such is *What If... Collected Thought Experiments in Philosophy*, by Peg Tittle (Harlow: Longman, 2004).

A Sneetch Is a Sneetch and Other Philosophical Discoveries: Finding Wisdom in Children's Literature, First Edition. Thomas E. Wartenberg. Illustrations © Joy Kinigstein.
© 2013 John Wiley & Sons, Inc. Published 2013 by John Wiley & Sons, Inc.

There are also more content-specific introductions to philosophy from various publishers. I can't help mentioning my own *Existentialism: A Beginner's Guide* (Oxford: Oneworld, 2008) that provides an accessible but rigorous introduction to this philosophical school. It's one in a series of *Beginner's Guides* published by Oneworld, some of which are focused on philosophy. There are also a series of *Very Short Introductions* (Oxford: Oxford University Press) to various areas of philosophy.

There is also a number of book series from different publishers that look at various items in popular culture from a philosophical point of view. One that I edited is called *Fight Club (Philosophers on Film)* (Abingdon: Routledge, 2011). Many have the form of *X and Philosophy*, where X is a movie, book, or television show.

Audio Material

If you prefer listening to reading, you're in luck. Many books, including my *Existentialism: A Beginner's Guide* (Oxford: Oneworld, 2012) are available as audio books. Check to see if others of the books listed above are available in that format.

Philosophy Talk (www.philosophytalk.org) is a radio show that focuses each week on different philosophical issues. Entertaining, but also a great way to learn about philosophy.

The Web

Wikipedia has entries on virtually every philosophical issue you can think of, though you have to be careful about the accuracy of what they contain.

There are two internet encyclopedias specifically devoted to philosophy. Both are peer-reviewed, meaning that the entries have been checked for accuracy by professional philosophers.

The Internet Encyclopedia of Philosophy (www.iep.utm.edu)

The Stanford Encyclopedia of Philosophy (http://plato.stanford.edu). The entries here are written by philosophers for philosophers, but are quite good if sometimes a bit abstract.

Philosophy Compass (http://onlinelibrary.wiley.com/journal/10.1111 /(ISSN)1747-9991) has good introductions to many philosophical areas and questions.